# ESCAPE _to_ GOD

## A DESPERATE SEARCH FOR HIS PRESENCE

JIM HOHNBERGER
WITH TIM AND JULIE CANUTESON

THOMAS NELSON
*Since 1798*

NASHVILLE   DALLAS   MEXICO CITY   RIO DE JANEIRO   BEIJING

Published in Nashville, Tennessee. Thomas Nelson is a trademark of Thomas Nelson, Inc.

Thomas Nelson, Inc. titles may be purchased in bulk for educational, business, fundraising, or sales promotional use. For information, please e-mail SpecialMarkets @ThomasNelson.com.

All Scripture quotations, unless otherwise indicated, are taken from the New King James Version® (NKJV). Copyright © 1982 by Thomas Nelson, Inc. Used by permission. All rights reserved.

Scriptures marked KJV are from the King James Version of the Bible.

A note to the reader: Every experience shared in this volume is true although, in a few cases, multiple individuals have been combined into one character for sake of brevity and clarity. In most cases, the names, locations, and other unimportant characteristics have been altered to protect the privacy of the individuals involved. Outside of those whose names and stories have been used with their permission, resemblance to any person or persons, outside of the author and his family, is strictly coincidental.

### Library of Congress Cataloging-in-Publication Data

Hohnberger, Jim, 1948-
　　　Escape to God : a desperate search for His presence / Jim Hohnberger with Tim and Julie Canuteson.
　　　　p. cm.
　　　Originally published : Nampa, Idaho : Pacific Press Pub., c2001.
　　　ISBN 10: 0-7852-8897-X (trade paper)
　　　ISBN 13: 978-0-7852-8897-8 (trade paper)
　　　ISBN 0-7852-1447-X (hardcover)
　　　1. Hohnberger, Jim, 1948- 2. Seventh-Day Adventists—United States—
Biography. I. Canuteson, Tim, 1963- II. Canuteson, Julie, 1967- III. Title.
　　　BX6193.H63A3 2006
　　　286.7092—dc22

2005026121

*Printed in the United States of America*

07 08 09 10 RRD 9 8 7 6 5 4 3 2 1

To all those in this hour of Earth's history whose religious lives are marked by a growing hunger and thirst after God Himself and will not be satisfied until they have learned to daily walk with their Master.

# CONTENTS

*Chapter One*

# THE GLORIOUS PURSUIT

It shall come to pass
That before they call, I will answer.
*Isaiah 65:24 NKJV*

"JIM, WHAT ARE you doing way up here anyway?" Warren asked.

I could read his thoughts. Clearly he was convinced that I was wasting my life in the mountains when I could be making big money down in the city. Warren had come to look for wilderness property, and, even now, Warren, his pregnant wife, and I were bumping over backcountry roads in my truck to look at a piece of land for them.

"Well, Warren," I began, "you see, I'm a Christian, and we came here because—"

"Stop right there, Jim!" Warren cut me off. "I'm not a Christian, and I don't believe in Christianity. I don't want to hear another word about it!"

The sudden hostility was unmistakable in the close confines of my vehicle. *How can God reach a person like this?* I thought. Nonetheless I felt constrained to say something more, and with a

1

silent prayer I responded, "Warren, all I need is a couple of minutes of your time, and I will never say another word about Christianity. Warren, the God I've come to know in these mountains loves you so much that even though you are rejecting Him, someday when you need Him, He will be there for you. Someday you're going to need my God!"

If things were cold in my truck before, after those words they were downright frigid. It seemed I had made things even worse with my comments. We finished our business and Warren drove off, but the memory of our conversation reminded me of my own estrangement from God. The echo of my own words rang in my ears: "Someday when you need Him, He will be there for you. Someday you're going to need my God."

## MEMORIES

I certainly wasn't raised understanding my need for God, although my family did consider themselves Christians. When did I start pursuing God? As I reflect back over my life, I realize this might well be the wrong question to ask, for I was not the pursuer, but let me start at the beginning.

The stories my family tells of my birth come vividly to mind, and they run something like this:

"Sir," said a tired-looking doctor to get the attention of a man who appeared, if possible, to be more tired and worried than the physician.

"Yes?" Henry responded hopefully. His response seemed out of character in the worn waiting room with its lingering smell of tobacco smoke and the ever-present scent of fear and expectation, which haunts such rooms.

"It's a boy!" A ghost of a smile danced about the physician's sturdy face. "A nine-pound, five-ounce baby boy!"

"How's my wife?" Henry asked, already animated with the news of his son.

"It was a hard delivery." Concern was evident in the expert's face. "You may see her now," he answered before the question was asked.

My parents always looked at each other in a special way at this point in the story, and all of us understood both that the situation had been difficult and that the crisis had drawn them together even closer.

Reminiscing, I realize that as I lay in my mother's arms, I had no idea that at birth I had become a participant in the great conflict between God and Satan. Only much later would I come to see that even as I lay in the womb, God, in His infinite wisdom, had set in motion an individualized plan to awaken in my heart a longing, a need for Him. He knew I was being born into a world that was at odds with Him, in rebellion to His principles, His will, and His ways.

God knew I was to be born with a nature damaged by man's experimentation with sin. God also knew I would naturally follow my own impulses and inclinations and that the very thought of yielding my will and way to Him would be totally foreign to me. He knew all too well that Satan would oppose every effort He made to pursue me. In spite of these odds, God set His plans for me in motion.

After waiting thousands of years for Jim Hohnberger to be born, He now had the opportunity to try to win my love. God was in pursuit of me as He is every one of us. It is a glorious pursuit of love, born out of the heart of God.

My parents, Bernice and Henry Hohnberger, were pleased with me, their third child, and they took me home to their modest house in Appleton, Wisconsin, determined to do all they could to see I grew up to be an honest worker and a good citizen. As an infant, I had no conception of a loving God, but God still was speaking to me through my parents. They taught me my first lessons about the character of God through their interactions with me.

Parents stand in the place of God to young children, and by obeying parents they learn to obey God. Thus began the great tug-of-war in my life, in childish conflicts with my parents. As my selfish will made its demands, my parents either gave in and allowed some indulgence or stopped me from demanding my own way. At the time, none of us fully understood the implications—sometimes Satan won a conflict and sometimes God did—but always I was growing and learning.

Inside each of us from birth is the desire to find fulfillment and happiness. Unless guided by wise parents and the grace of God, this all too often means that we seek fulfillment in things. Things are not wrong, for when God made the earth, He filled it with things that bring pleasure, but the temptation is everlasting for people to place value upon the things rather than the One who is the Giver of such things.

Think back over your own experiences of Christmases past. After tearing the gaily colored ribbon and paper away to find some desired toy, you could scarcely express thanks to the one who had given such a gift. Perhaps you mumbled a few words of thanks under your mother's prompting, but all your eyes could see was the treasured possession. The possession had taken the place of the giver.

For me, it was my new double-chrome-plated, three-speed Schwinn bicycle. Oh, how I loved that bike! It was the finest in the neighborhood. Eventually, that love evolved into an affair with a fire-engine-red Pontiac convertible. I was slowly being trained by the world about me to equate happiness with the things I possessed.

*Things* consist not only of possessions, but positions, people, power, pride, and pleasure as well. Multitudes believe happiness and fulfillment come from attaining a prominent position invested with power and pride. Still others believe that being married to a certain person or visiting exotic locations will bring lasting joy. Others desire a life of pleasure seeking and freedom from responsibility, hoping that this will bring true happiness.

All these things become a real source of competition for the affections of our hearts, which are what God desires. God sees all this, and His pursuit of us begins before we even have a desire to find fulfillment in Him: "Before they call, I will answer" (Isa. 65:24 NKJV).

Praise God that He plants within our hearts a desire for true fulfillment that the world's methods can but dimly satisfy. There are evidences all around us of apparently successful people who have found wealth, power, and fame—everything that the world says should bring happiness. Yet these are some of the most miserable people on earth, and they often end their own lives in the wretchedness of drug-induced suicides.

In this controversy for human souls, the devil uses all the world's glitter and gold to seduce us. His methods use deception to make even our worst choices look good. But in this battle for our hearts, God never lies. He never misleads. He says, "Behold, I stand at the door and knock. If anyone hears My voice and opens the door, I will come in to him and dine with him, and he with Me" (Rev. 3:20 NKJV).

God appeals to our intellect, our reason, and our conscience. Our response has to be voluntary. He doesn't want robots. God has placed a desire for Him within our hearts, but our response to that desire is entirely up to us. God never forces our will.

I didn't know I had a problem with self wanting its own way. It was all I had ever known. Still God pursued and courted me for thirty years until I finally felt my need of Him. While I will describe the process more fully in the chapters that follow, I want you to understand that God does not give up on us. It took another ten years until He had gained my affections, and then another six or so years until I finally surrendered the citadel of my heart and was His. This doesn't invalidate my earlier experiences with God, but instead demonstrates that for most of us, the process of change is gradual, and it took me years to move from my first responses to God's pursuit to a wholehearted surrender to His love.

As I gradually moved toward becoming a surrendered Christian, I found my past experiences hindered me to the extent that I easily fell back into the old habits of trying to find fulfillment in the things I had, rather than in an experience with Christ. I honestly thought that intellectual assent to truth was what constituted being a Christian, and the more knowledge I had and the more closely my life matched my idealistic concepts of the way a real Christian lived, the more I was becoming a better Christian.

## MY DREAM PROPERTY

One of the ideas I had garnered from my study at that time was that the closer we could live to God's ideal for man when he was created, the better our lives would be. God placed Adam and Eve in the Garden of Eden. Therefore, I longed for real country living.

When an acquaintance offered me a chance to visit his country estate, I toured the woodlands, fields, and garden area with delight. He was justly proud of his place, and I couldn't help telling him, "If you ever decide to sell, I want to have the first opportunity to purchase."

"That's awful nice of you to say, Jim, but I'm never going to sell it."

"That may be, but I'm serious. If you ever sell, I want the first opportunity to purchase."

"Jim, I am *never* selling . . . But all right, I'll give you first shot if anything ever changes."

About five months later, he called me at the end of a week. "Jim, you'll never believe what's happened. I've been offered a dream job. The only problem is I have to relocate to Madison. You wanted the first opportunity to buy my place—well, it's yours. Be at my place tomorrow morning at ten, and we'll see what we can work out. A lot of people want this place, and I have to leave quickly, so you will need to decide fast!"

I automatically agreed to meet, my spirits soaring with the idea of owning such a property and then dropping like a rock when I realized that the next day I was to be in church. I couldn't bring myself to conduct a business deal on the one day I devoted to worship. I wanted that ideal property so badly. I wanted it because I thought it was what God wanted for my family, but I didn't conduct business on my day of worship.

In my mind, I struggled over and over with what to do. What kind of deal could God work out if I refused to negotiate? Could I trust Him even if I missed out on the property?

The next day, I decided to show up a little late for church. After this man's kindness in offering the property to me first, I felt I couldn't cancel on him in an impersonal manner over the phone. With my more mature understanding today, I wouldn't have tried to conduct any business on my day of worship, but in my understandings then, even refusing to negotiate was a huge step of faith for me. I was at his house a few minutes before ten. He was all smiles until I told him I wasn't willing to negotiate that day due to my religious convictions. I told him, "I'm sorry, but I'll just have to let this opportunity go by."

"Jim," he responded, "I would never want to get between you and your religion. When would you be willing to meet?"

I don't know why, when we want God to work a miracle for us, we are so shocked when He does. My friend's willingness to delay astounded me. I knew many people wanted his place. I would have been even more shocked had I known that all along he was sure I couldn't afford it, and he was just fulfilling his word. Under those conditions, it was an extraordinarily kind and noble deed that spoke volumes about his character.

After suggesting we meet on Monday, I spent a rather stimulated Sunday anticipating the next day's activities. When we met, we came to terms rather easily, but he needed a five-thousand-dollar binder to accept the offer. The problem was I didn't have it, but I wrote him the check anyway. Then I went home and called the manager of the bank and told him what I'd done. "So you see, Stanley," I concluded, "I need your help."

"I'll say you do. He's here, by the way. He just presented the check to one of the cashiers. In fact, she just brought it back to me wondering what to do."

I was in a panic. I had planned on having a day or two to get things worked out. I had a great business relationship with the bank and did all my personal and business banking with them. I even insured the bank president and counted him a friend, so I really didn't think there'd be a problem, but I hadn't planned on the seller being quite this eager. There was the world's longest pause while the banker let me sweat, then he said, "Don't worry, we will honor the check."

This was one of the first times in my life I placed God higher than something I wanted. In so doing, I began to understand that God does not want our things, but if those things have usurped the throne of our hearts, they must be dethroned. God wanted to provide me the property I desired, but oh, how much more He wanted me to trust Him in a personal and intimate way. He was teaching me that even though I had but a tiny bit of knowledge about following Him and even though I was trying to follow Him in a very legalistic, doctrinal way, rather than in a surrendered relationship, when I needed Him, when the chips were down, He was going to be there for me.

We often hesitate to give up our things to the Lord out of fear for their safety. This is especially true when those treasures are long-cherished idols. But we need have no such fears. Jesus came not to destroy but to save. Everything is safe when we commit it to Him, and nothing is really safe if we don't.

## SIX MONTHS LATER

I was traveling in the Midwest. While I was visiting with a family, the phone rang. The woman of the house said, "Jim, it's for you."

"Hi, Jim. It's me, Warren."

"Warren," I almost shouted, my mind traveling back to our conversation in the truck. "How did you ever find me out here?"

"It wasn't easy," he said. Suddenly the self-confident voice changed as he said, "We had that baby, Jim."

"Wonderful! What did you have?"

"I had a son . . ." his voice trailed off.

"What's the matter, Warren?" I asked.

"Jim," he said, with anguish in his voice, "my son was born with three holes in his heart. I need your God, Jim! I need your God!"

Warren's need had swept aside his anger and fear. His story brought tears to my eyes as I was privileged to share with Warren the glad news of God's glorious pursuit for every human heart.

When I first asked my future wife, Sally, out on a date, her potential responses were limited: she could accept or refuse. To be sure, to accept carried more risk. But to refuse would have been to forgo a lifetime of sharing the joy of a heart in tune with hers and a marriage made in heaven. What a sad alternative that would have been!

And so it is in this glorious pursuit of a loving God for the throne of our hearts. There are not a dozen possible responses—just one good choice and one very poor alternative. My choice has been to pick up that pursuit, which will not end till I stand face-to-face with the one I have come to know and love.

# Chapter Two

# RELIGION—IS IT ENOUGH?

And this is eternal life, that they may know You, the only
true God, and Jesus Christ whom You have sent.
*John 17:3 NKJV*

"BUT MOM, DO I have to go? I don't like going to church. I never
get anything out of it." It was a beautiful Sunday morning, and I
hated to waste it. Of course, my mother refused my plea, and I
found my unwilling self attending church, just as I had every weekend of my whole life.

I wasn't kidding when I said I never got anything out of it and
as far as I could see, no one else did either! My mother was Catholic,
and my father was Lutheran. Father rarely attended church, while
Mother went every week; however, both believed in church attendance for us kids in much the same way they believed in hard work,
dependability, and high moral standards. I could easily see how the
latter principles affected their lives in a positive way, but church
attendance? It was more like something we put on and took off at
the door of the church.

Even though my father was not a regular church attendee, I

knew his character. I remember the time my father had a dehumidifier installed in late summer. It worked perfectly, and we never gave it a second thought until spring. One evening at the dinner table, my father asked my mother, "Bernice, have we ever gotten a bill for that dehumidifier?"

Mother looked thoughtful for a moment before replying. "No, I don't believe we have."

I was in my early teens at this point, and I could put two and two together. "Guess we got us a free dehumidifier!" I sang out.

My father just looked at me, a strange mix of disappointment and shock on his face, as if I had uttered a profanity. My father said nothing, though; he just walked over to the phone and called the company. "This is Henry Hohnberger," I heard him say. "You installed a dehumidifier for us last summer, and we haven't received a bill. Yes . . . yes. That would be fine."

He hung up and returned to the table. "They said they'll mail a bill out this week. Somehow it slipped through the system. The secretary said that if I hadn't called, they would never have known."

It was a vivid lesson in honesty, and I have never forgotten it. In the same way, I saw that the principles they believed about hard work and dependability were an integral part of their lives too. My father and mother worked hard every day. They were never late and so scheduled you could have set your watch to the rhythms of their lives. Yet church attendance, which was all I understood of religion, did not have this same type of practical, parental demonstration of life application.

Perhaps this is not too surprising. The differences between Protestantism and Catholicism separated my parents. They got along by keeping religion a quiet and private thing, never discussed and never verbalized, although both felt that going to church was good for us kids. They were even flexible to the point of allowing us older kids a choice of which services we attended, but the church service and religion as a whole were not a part of our daily lives.

This lack of practical application to my life made church such a burden to me that I must confess there were times I took advantage of this freedom to attend different services. I would sneak into the back of the church, grab a bulletin, and quickly leave for the park to while away the hour, then arrive back at home with the evidence of my attendance, never fearing that I might be questioned about the service's content.

It's not that my parents didn't try. They sent me to Christian schools and made sure I attended church every week, but somehow religion was just too artificial, too formal, too boring to reach me. I had to attend, so I learned at an early age to play the game, so to speak. You probably know it yourself and not because you were a member of my church watching me. Many professed Christians go through the motions, doing what is expected—looking good on the outside but knowing their hearts are just not in it. They may not even be able to explain it, but it's just not meeting their true needs; and yet they follow suit because, well, it's the "right" thing to do.

When I was out from under my loving parents' influence, I quit attending. I pursued my own interests. I had had enough of going to church and acting religious. When I added it all up, it amounted to no saving good anyway. God was no more real to me than He was to my non-Christian friends.

My father had been a good, moral man, apart from organized religion, and I didn't see why I couldn't be the same. So I went my own way, and God waited for the right moment to get my attention—so He could introduce me to something better.

## DISCOVERY

I was thirty years old. I had graduated from college and spent five years selling computer systems, and I was now the sole proprietor of the Hohnberger Agency—a multi-line insurance agency specializing in automobile, homeowner's, life, and health insurance. I was young and aggressive, building a future, a retirement, and a comfortable present. I was "making it" in the world. I had a lovely home, new vehicles, a good income, and a prospering business. I was chasing the American dream, believing that happiness came from the things that made life interesting, comfortable, and exciting.

I was also more troubled by the course I was following than I cared to admit.

The problem wasn't worldly success. I was delighted with how much we had achieved at a relatively young age. The problem was that my wife, Sally, and I were beginning to question what that success was costing us. Something elemental was missing; our relationship with each other was slowly eroding. If you had asked me, I would never have said that religion was the answer—I'd already been religious, and it had gotten me nowhere. Both of us were deeply troubled by this unfulfilled "something," but we didn't dwell on it amid the busyness of life that demanded our immediate attention.

I liked to be at the office before anyone else got there, but increasingly I found myself stuck in traffic, breathing in the fumes of the truck in front of me while I restlessly tapped my fingers on the steering wheel, impatient at the delay. Even little things irritated me. "Who do you think you are?" I found myself muttering when a young woman scooted into the very parking spot I was waiting for, forcing me to park in the *second* row! By the time I got to my office, I was already more than a little stressed. Nevertheless, I made sure I treated each of my employees and clients with the utmost courtesy and respect. My parents' influence and insistence on proper manners and behavior paid off there. It was just a habit.

As I got into my car to head home, I was dead tired. My neck hurt from the tension that had been building all day long. I felt cranky and tired. All I wanted to do was get home and vegetate in front of the TV, and that was exactly what I was going to do just as soon as I could make my way around the smelly old bus in front of me. *Rats! If only I had gotten out a few minutes earlier,* I fumed.

Meanwhile, at home Sally had waited all day for my sympathy, understanding, and companionship. She worked hard to raise our little boy, Matthew. She had given up nursing, a career she loved, to stay home with our child. I admired her choice in an intellectual way but really had no concept of what she did all day. Oh, I knew she had the house to maintain, meals to make, and shopping to do, not to mention Matthew to care for—and he wasn't the easiest little whippersnapper to deal with. But surely that couldn't be any harder than dealing with irate, picky clients all day long.

Once inside the house, I headed right for my chair. Putting my feet up and closing my eyes, I started to relax. Then Sally came in and started telling me about her struggle with Matthew's nap time. "Jim, I can't get him to go to sleep. He sits in there and plays. I know he's tired."

"Sally," I snapped, "you are older than him, smarter than him, and bigger than him. You outweigh him ten to one. *Just make him!*" I yelled. "This is ridiculous!" I knew I had said the wrong thing, handled it the wrong way, but right then I was just too tired to care.

But I couldn't escape my thoughts. When we were dating, Sally was all I ever needed or wanted, all I had lived for. Whatever troubled her troubled me. We were one. What had happened to us in just a few short years? Why had she become a comfortable convenience rather than the special someone in my life?

Solomon, the wisest man who ever lived, summed it up so well when he said, "All is vanity" (Eccl. 1:2 NKJV). Vanity is emptiness, a mirage, something you can never get your hands on. I was pursuing this emptiness, this American myth, and God needed to get my attention.

God knew the pressures building up in my life, and He longed to help me, so some months before He had prompted me to sell life insurance to my dentist. Little did I know how drastically my life was going to change from following that one divine prompting.

My dentist was one of my clients. I insured his business, his home, his health, and his auto, so I couldn't see why I shouldn't sell him some life insurance too. I made an appointment with him one day to do just that. He wasn't interested, which made no sense to me as I knew he was a reasonable man. "Why don't you want to purchase this life insurance plan?" I asked.

"Because I believe the Lord is going to return before I would need or benefit from such coverage," he responded.

I laughed at him! Out loud! You hear all kinds of excuses in the insurance business, but this was *absurd*. I thought he must be joking. "What's the real reason?" I probed.

"That is the real reason."

"Where did you ever get that idea?"

"From the Bible. Don't you ever read the Bible, Jim?"

"The Bible! Why that's just a bunch of 'Our Fathers' and 'Hail Marys'!"

"Oh nooo, it's not."

So began an hour-and-a-half discussion, not on life insurance but on life assurance. My interest was stirred and my curiosity aroused. This was a side of religion I had never seen before. He looked at his watch and said, "Jim, I have to get home. I have obligations. Why don't you and your wife come over Wednesday evening, and we can continue our discussion then?"

"I can ask you anything, and you won't be offended?"

"Of course," he assured me.

"Sounds great!" I said. "We'll be there!"

Of course, I hadn't cleared it yet with Sally, but not many months earlier she had mentioned the idea of attending church services with one of the nurses she worked with. I had exploded at the very idea of religion. My strong reaction had stopped her from pursuing the idea, but she had grown up singing in the choir and missed it, so I felt she probably wouldn't object too strenuously. I was right. She said, "Sure, Jim, I'll give it a try," making me feel doubly bad about my outburst at her suggestion.

This was how we started out: both of us hurting, both of us too hassled and too hurried by the life we were living.

Wednesday evening, Paul and Ethel Conner greeted us warmly. After a few minutes of our visiting in their living room, Paul suggested we move to the dining room where the four of us sat around the large table. I contemplated how strange these people were. My entire adult social life revolved around alcohol, and offering someone a drink was how you showed you were hospitable, but this quiet couple didn't offer us a beer. At the time, I didn't realize God was using them to show me a better form of hospitality, not one in an open bottle but in an open and welcoming heart. Paul excused himself to get something. I thought maybe he had belatedly remembered the beer, but *no,* he walked around the corner with four, count them, one, two, three, four Bibles! *Oh no!* I thought. *He must be some kind of fanatic. Even the pope doesn't own four Bibles!*

Then he proceeded to pass them out and said, "Jim, open your Bible to Daniel."

"What's Daniel?" I asked.

"That's a book in the Old Testament."

"What's the Old Testament?"

"You really weren't kidding when you said you didn't read the Bible," Paul said with a smile.

I must confess, I had very little interest in studying the Bible, and when he brought out the four books, I was all set to head out the door after a couple of minutes—unless something he shared really caught my attention. And it did! Sally and I left their house at 11:30 that night. We had never heard such startling concepts in all our lives.

I had honestly thought the Bible was simply a collection of prayers and maybe a story or two. Before that night, I had never held a Bible in my hands, let alone read one, so I was more than a little shocked when Paul showed me that the Bible was a book of history, of real-life concepts, and of prophecy. I was amazed to see that the Bible demonstrated the history of God's church and was an extraordinary display of logic, order, and wisdom.

These ideas may seem very basic and obvious to you, but for me it was an astonishing revelation. That night I glimpsed something that I could use to order my life and perhaps find the fulfillment I had been seeking for so long. The truths rang the bell in my heart that would eventually awaken the desire God had planted there for Him.

They invited us to come again the next week. I started to look forward to Wednesday night. Paul was a real scholar. He made the Bible come alive by removing it from the world of speculation or theory and placing it in the context of history. When Paul told me what he believed, he could show me in the Bible why he believed it.

This was novel and exciting to me. I was enthralled at what we were learning, and Sally, who had longed for some spiritual involvement in our home, especially now that we were expecting a child, was delighted to see her husband suddenly interested in religion.

We continued our Bible studies with the Conners every Wednesday evening for the next eighteen months. I had no idea the Bible contained such truths. Periodically, at the end of a study, Ethel asked, "Jim, how about coming to church this weekend?"

"No, not until I am absolutely convinced that this is truth," I always said. That response had almost become a tradition for us, so her face registered shock one week when I announced, "This weekend I am going to church. I can't wait to meet the saints who are living this kind of truth!"

I was excited! This was going to be a big thrill, for if these truths had excited me, then surely meeting those who were living out these truths would be a wonderful event. Paul and Ethel didn't seem quite as excited as I was. In fact, they looked a little uncomfortable.

"Jim," Ethel said hesitantly, "there are a few things we need to tell you before you go to church . . ."

Well, they tried to tell me what I would quickly find out for myself: not all the "saints" are saints. Later, I would find the Bible speaks of this by saying: "For they are not all Israel who are of Israel" (Rom. 9:6 NKJV). "For he is not a Jew who is one outwardly . . . but he is a Jew who is one inwardly" (Rom. 2:28–29 NKJV). Strong words, but little did I realize how soon they would apply to me.

During those eighteen months of study, I began a love affair with God's Word. God was using His Word to awaken in my heart a response toward Him. I fell, however, into one of the traps Satan lays for those seeking God. I felt that intellectual assent to the truth was all that constituted becoming a Christian. I truly believed, so much so that the truths contained in His Word became my religion.

I had longed all my life for someone to show me how to be a Christian, and now I felt I had found the way. I didn't understand it at the time, but my early experiences with church and religion had created in me the mind-set that you did things because they were the "right" things to do—they were what other "religious" people expected of me. I had no idea this would color my religious understanding for many years to come and hinder me severely in my journey toward God.

This tendency to "right doing" clouded my vision and kept me from seeing that the externals of religion ought to be an outgrowth of an inward experience, not the *essence* of the experience. I had a strong will, and as I discovered truths in God's Word, I rapidly applied them to my life, assuming that made me even more religious.

I had zeal for my truths. That's for sure. I was sincere. I was honest. I was also dead wrong about what constitutes becoming a Christian.

## ZEALOT!

My zeal led me to try to share with my family the wonderful "truths" I was discovering. As I tried to show them that their doctrinal positions were not biblical, they didn't like it. They wouldn't accept my truths. Oh, they may not have been able to provide an explanation or defend their positions biblically, but they refused to accept mine. This was baffling to me. I thought that surely when they were convinced of the "truth," they would want to obey it.

I went back again and again, with even more zeal, until my family made it clear that not only did they not want to have anything to do with my new religion, but they really didn't care if they had anything to do with me either. My attitude stated clearly, "I'm right, and you're wrong. I have the truth, and you believe a lie." It totally turned them off, and rightly so.

I had embraced a system of truths and was delighted to find out what the Bible taught, but in my zeal for truth, I was also unaware that I had missed the essence of Christianity. Too many years have passed for me to say exactly how it happened, but somehow I never grasped the idea that Christianity involved a vital, on-going, ever-deepening connection with Christ.

Others noticed my zeal for outreach, and soon I was giving Bible studies to other earnest souls, who, just like myself, accepted the wonderful truths of the Bible as their religion rather than Him to whom the truths point. I became the head elder in the local church and looked good on the outside.

It became increasingly clear, however, even to this stubborn German, that something in this Christian life I was leading was not quite right. I could go to church and present a beautiful message about overcoming sin, yet I couldn't live it.

## JUST LEAVE ME ALONE!

It had been another one of those days at the office that left me so beat that I headed for the recliner as soon as I hit the door. I plopped down, and the next thing I knew, there was a warm little body as close to mine as he could get. It was Matthew. He was a little older by this time, no longer a baby, but still very much a little boy, gleefully holding a childishly wrapped box.

I didn't know it, but during the day, he and Sally had been talking about my birthday coming up in just four days. This excited his four-year-old imagination, so he got busy and gathered up some "treasures." Then he colored and pasted a few more. Before long, they were all wrapped in the box, my present, and after waiting all day for me to come home, he just couldn't wait another minute to give it to me.

He stood by my chair, almost bouncing in his excitement. He had poured out his little heart in love for his father and was as thrilled with my gift as he had ever been with one of his own birthday presents. "Father, Father, I have a birthday present for you!"

"Not now, Matthew!"

"But Father—"

"I'm tired."

"But Father—"

"No! Just leave me alone. I'm tired, and besides," I snarled, "it's not my birthday!" The little face that had been the picture of excitement moments before fell. I had crushed his joy and wounded his spirit, and he turned away to find Sally and comfort.

I sat back in my chair and tried to rest, feeling miserable. Why couldn't I control myself? My lack of self-control was my one big problem in living the Christian life. I could act like a Christian at church, and then I could go home, yell at my wife, and get irritated at my children. I knew this was not right, but even with my strong human willpower, I couldn't seem to gain victory in this area.

The Bible describes it like this: "Out of the same mouth proceed blessing and cursing. My brethren, these things ought not to be so. Does a spring send forth fresh water and bitter from the same opening? . . . Thus no spring yields both salt water and fresh" (James 3:10–12 NKJV). "If anyone among you thinks he is religious, and does not bridle his tongue but deceives his own heart, this one's religion is useless" (James 1:26 NKJV).

The Lord began to speak to me in such texts, and a nagging suspicion started taking hold in my mind. *Maybe I've missed something. Am I really what I think I am?* I was in the church, but was I in Christ? I was in the Word, but was I in the Word that was made flesh and dwelt among us?

It dawned on me that just because a mouse is in the cookie jar, it doesn't make him a cookie! Over a couple of years, the Lord finally got through my stubborn spirit and said, "Jim, you need to pull back and reassess what you're doing. You need to make sure you're converted, not just in your mental choice for Me as your Savior but in your actions."

"Me? Why, Lord, I'm the head elder of the church! I've brought more than a dozen people into Your church. Me? Is it possible that I am not fully converted? Lord, can it be that in spite of all the changes You have brought into my life, there is a greater, a deeper, a better experience in You that I haven't yet grasped?"

"Yes, Jim, there are some things you just don't understand— and you are not alone. Many who have taken My name do not realize the full extent of the salvation I design them to experience."

So I began my new odyssey of seeking out the deeper life beyond the basics of Christianity. I came to understand that orthodoxy or right doctrinal opinions are but a slender part of true religion. Today there are millions of professed Christians who hold "right" opinions. Today millions have embraced Christianity and, just as I did, have made reforms. Yet today, in millions of homes, Christianity has not prevented us from hurting those we love with our words. Could it be that our religion is as the Bible describes it—"in vain"? This was my experience. For the first time in my life, I was actively and willingly participating in the church, yet, in spite of all I had learned, my own life-transforming spirituality was at low ebb.

Sound biblical exposition is an absolute must for any Christian to survive the great events at the close of Earth's history. Yet we may carry on the exposition in such a way that we lead the hearers into a system of "truths" rather than leading them to God. This is what had happened to me in my studies.

You see, it is not mere words that revive the soul, but God Himself, and until the hearers find God in a personal experience, they are not always better for having merely heard "the truth." Knowledge is a wonderful thing, but the old saying that a little knowledge is a dangerous thing is true in the realm of spiritual things. What I failed to grasp in my limited understanding of God was that the Bible is not an end in itself, but a means, a tool to bring people to an intimate walk with their God. It was knowledge of God in a deep and intimate relationship, rather than knowledge about the things of God, that I was missing.

I know I am not the only one who has fallen into this error, for Jesus spoke to the church in His day, stating, "You search the Scriptures, for in them you think you have eternal life; and these are they which testify of Me. But you are not willing to come to Me that you may have life" (John 5:39–40 NKJV).

These words have been preserved to this day for our benefit, and we should consider their meaning. The temptation is ever before us to accept the forms of religion and miss its very essence without ever realizing our true condition.

I had theological understanding and could discuss my biblical exposition in learned terms, but if I had come face-to-face with true, living Christianity, my great knowledge would have appeared as foolishness. If I could have stood at the foot of the cross and talked with Mary Magdalene, what would our conversation have been like? I would have known all the proper theological terms, but if I had tried to use them with her, she would have said, "What? Who? Whatever are you talking about? I love Him! He's my Lord, my Savior! He redeemed me! He loved me when no one else would."

In that case, which one of us would have had true religion: the head elder or the harlot? I had all the right terms, but she would have had the heart experience.

## CHURCHIANITY

Organized religion may prove to be the greatest substitute for a saving knowledge of God that the world has ever known. A great danger lies in complacency. We may have accepted the doctrines and attend weekly services, which makes us feel content that we are safely in the fold. After all, we are in the church and in His Word, so we conclude we must have found God. I did!

Only much later would I come to understand that some of the darkest chapters of human history are the almost unspeakable cruelties religious men committed to defend their understandings of truth. I took it for granted that I was a Christian because I believed in certain theological concepts, but I knew little about the love of God and had no power to transform my life in those areas that really mattered. Profession of truth does not make us kind, patient, or godly.

Church membership and a profession of faith have wrongly

become synonymous with the new-birth experience, but because everyone about us has approximately the same experience we possess, we see no danger and sense no need of a deeper experience. This situation exists to some degree in nearly all churches and denominations of our day. The spurious belief that we have found religion through knowledge, profession, and attendance alone allows us to treat God as a convenience rather than the nucleus of our everyday lives.

It may sound as though I am against religion, but this is not so. While organized religion did not bring me to God, it was a springboard, a stimulus that opened my eyes and started me thinking. What organized religion taught me has been a catalyst, if you will, to point me in a direction, to ground me in some principles, and to provide me with some structure in understanding the Word of God. Without this, few would ever enter the path to a deeper life.

But I long for all people, in the church or out, to see what has been forgotten in our day and age: that God is a Person whom all can know and experience. I wish that somehow, when I was studying the truths of God's Word, that I had also learned that intercourse between God and the soul is the heartbeat of the true Christian experience! Daily, hourly, moment by moment, God directing, God empowering, God inspiring us to live a "life . . . hid with Christ in God" (Col. 3:3 KJV) that "God may be all in all" (1 Cor. 15:28 NKJV).

I had read in the Bible about people like Enoch and David, who walked and talked with God. I wanted to obtain this same intimacy with God. Intuitively, I sensed this was the experience I had been missing in all that I had learned and seen. I didn't understand it, but somehow I longed for it in my deepest soul.

God put that longing in my heart, and He wanted to give me that experience, but He knew it was going to require some major changes in my life. God knew I would never find Him amid the "churchianity" and religiosity of the world, with its pride, pompous pretense, and self-promotion. So He gave me the same message Jesus gave His disciples. He said, "Come ye yourselves apart . . . and rest a while" (Mark 6:31 KJV).

He was giving me the very first keys to this experience. While I hadn't known it, God had been engaged in a glorious pursuit to win my heart and my love. I had finally responded to His love and wanted to find Him. The Bible promises, "And you will seek Me and find Me, when you search for Me with all your heart" (Jer. 29:13 NKJV). I was determined to do just that.

I was so stressed, so hurried, and so pressed with the demands of life, of running my own business, and of maintaining a home that His call to me to rest made sense. I really was tired. On top of my other commitments, I was a church leader and was so busy doing "the Lord's work" that I had been too busy even to consider the idea that I was *too busy*—period. God was making this clear to me. "Jim, you must be willing to trim your schedule, reduce your never-ending commitments, simplify your life so you can 'be still, and know that I am God'" (Ps. 46:10 NKJV).

The time for change was coming, but I could never have dreamed of what awaited us as we strove amid all the stresses to find a life of quiet simplicity.

*Chapter Three*

# A LIFE OF SIMPLICITY

In returning and rest you shall be saved;
In quietness and confidence shall be your strength.
*Isaiah 30:15* NKJV

THEIR CONVENTION WAS the largest the world had ever seen. From every corner of the earth came the delegates, worried because, instead of destroying the competition, they themselves seemed in danger of destruction. That evening their extraordinary leader would deliver the keynote address. The delegates talked to each other in hushed tones and repeated the hope that if anyone could turn the situation around, that night's speaker could!

For as long as they could remember, he had been their leader. More than that, he was the one they all wanted to emulate. He had both their affections and their loyalty, and over the years he had become, in essence, their god.

Thundering applause spontaneously erupted from the delegates as he appeared before them and took his place at the podium. He looked out at the sea of eager, upturned faces, and, like a politician, he fed upon the crowd's approval. As the ovation calmed, he took a deep breath and began.

"Listen, you devils! You aren't going to keep the Christians from going to their churches. They are going to go! You can't prevent them from holding their doctrines or from saying their prayers. They are going to do it! We must change our tactics if we are to enjoy continued success.

"Time is the key, my friends. We can concede them their doctrines, their prayers, and their churchgoing if we can control their time. Time is the essential ingredient, for without this they will never find a saving connection with Jesus!" He spitefully spat out the last word.

Satan went on. "Let them think they are saved while we control their time, and they are ours just as surely as those who never set foot inside a church. How are we going to do this? Simple. Keep them busy in the nonessentials of life and invent unnumbered schemes to occupy their minds. Encourage them to spend, spend, spend and then work, work, work to pay for it. Fill their mailboxes with catalogs full of the most enticing offers. Follow these up with credit-card offers to pay for it all.

"Teach them that happiness comes from things, and induce the husbands to work eight, ten, twelve hours a day, six to seven days a week. Make them work two jobs if necessary. Make it appear a necessity for the wives to work. Tell them there is just no other way if they are going to maintain the lifestyles they want for their families. Then get the wives to work long, hard hours coupled with the home responsibilities so they have no energy left at the end of the day for their husbands or children.

"Overstimulate their minds so they cannot hear Jesus whispering to their consciences. Bombard their senses with music playing in every home, workplace, and store. Make sure that bad news hits them every day, wherever they turn. Use newspapers, magazines, radio, and television twenty-four hours a day.

"Corrupt the moral fabric of their marriages and their young people by placing sensual images that invite impure thoughts on billboards, in movies, on newspaper or magazine covers, and, of course, on television. Use TV talk shows to parade the most deviant members of society through their living rooms. Have them hungrily feast upon the sordid details of immoral behavior until they begin to see evil as just another alternative.

"Have them dwell on the trash, trivia, and trouble of the world. Detail the misdeeds of the rich and famous. Distract them from serious realities of life by vain hopes with sweepstakes, lotteries, and casinos. Fill their shelves with books, magazines, and still more books. These represent time, and more time spent here is less time spent with God.

"Fill their homes with computers and send them out on an electronic highway where we control most of the exits. Send them lots of e-mail. Bog them down in the spam of never-ending information. Give them laptop computers so they can always be at work.

"Make sure everyone has a pager, even children. Fill their days with phone calls. Give them cordless and cellular phones so it is easy to talk all the time. Make sure their answering machines run over with messages.

"Overwhelm the children with activities: sports programs in school and after school, dance, ballet, Scouts, clubs, music lessons, proms, and parties. Stress them out with increasing amounts of homework at earlier and earlier ages. Send them to preschool and early childhood programs; get them away from the parents' influence, and let them lead lives as separate from their parents' as possible, so by the time they are teenagers, they have nothing in common with Mom and Dad. Have them so stressed that they will respond to our encouragement to be sexually active, to use cigarettes, alcohol, or other drugs as an escape.

"Even in their recreation let them be excessive. Send them on expensive vacations. Have them go, go, go! Have them return from their recreation exhausted, disquieted, and unprepared for the coming week. Don't let them go out into nature. Send them to amusement parks, sporting events, concerts, and movies instead. Make this saying your motto: 'Vacation makes them tired enough to go back to work, and poor enough that they have to!'

"If they avoid these traps, use their own churches against them. Give them so many offices, responsibilities, and problems to deal with that their time is consumed in 'good' works. When they meet for spiritual fellowship, involve them in gossip and small talk so that they leave with troubled consciences and unsettled emotions.

"Bring crisis after crisis to their churches so they are kept so busy putting out fires that they have no time to kindle the flame of the gospel in their own hearts. Encourage them to study doctrines and evangelism. Let them attend great church conferences on outreach, training seminars, and leadership workshops.

"Clear the way for great interdenominational rallies seeking reformation. Be sure you get them to pay lip service to putting family first, to family values. Then get them involved with great social issues such as abortion. Let them have conservative lifestyles but, at all costs, and in any way possible, keep them from going to the Bible and to God as sinners in need of salvation, for if they do, all is lost to us.

"Time is our greatest weapon and our greatest friend, my colleagues. Let us use it wisely and let them sleep in their deceptions just a little longer. Then both the world and the church will be ours, and we will have won an everlasting victory. Go forth, my friends, to the victory!"

With both hands raised, Satan exhorted his minions: "On to victory! On to victory! On to victory!" Until at last, only the echo and results of this climactic meeting filter down to us today.

It was quite a convention! I may not have guessed all the details of the meeting, but you be the judge of the results. Evil angels went eagerly to their assignments, causing Christians everywhere to get busy, busy, busy, and to rush here and there. We are not living simple lives, my friends. Our lives are too congested. The whole system is overstimulated. Has the devil been successful at his scheme? The plan has worked beyond his wildest dreams.

Satan has managed to get the whole world aboard a fast moving train that gains speed with each passing day, and he is unwilling to slow that train down so that anyone can get off. I spent more than thirty years of my life on that train, unaware of the path I was traveling.

You see, we humans are remarkably adept at not seeing the obvious. This insight was coming, but it would take a combination of one of the world's best-known wilderness areas and a virtually unknown little lake to get us off that train.

## STRESS

Realizing that we needed some time away from the workaday world, Sally and I started planning what we called Time Out. In late June of 1982, we packed the kids in the station wagon and headed toward Michigan's Upper Peninsula to camp by the shore of Imp Lake.

Almost nobody was around at that time of year, and we set up camp and walked but a few feet from our camp to the lakeshore. Matthew, age five, and Andrew, age three, immediately started throwing stones into the water. While they were occupied, Sally and I sat on the beach and tried to relax. The rush was over.

I was on vacation for ten days of no problems, no phones, and no responsibilities outside of my family. Yet as I sat there on the beach, I felt as if my whole body were racing. I turned to Sally and said, "Honey, would you take my pulse?"

"Sure," she said, taking my wrist in her hand and reverting to her familiar role as a professional nurse. "It's eighty-eight."

"Is that good?" I asked.

"No, Jim," she said, her beautiful face clouded with concern. "That's not good for a man thirty-three years young who's just sitting on the beach."

A few days later, I was skipping stones on that same beach with my sons. They were admiring my efforts with an awe that only young children have for their father's accomplishments. I felt relaxed, refreshed, and calm.

"Honey, would you take my pulse?" I asked again. The result was sixty-eight. I was astonished! The math was easy. Just by relaxing, I had slowed my heart rate twenty beats per minute. That was a difference of almost twenty-nine thousand beats a day. It began to dawn on me just how much stress I was living under and what that stress was doing to my body.

This simple event set the tone for the rest of our vacation. What was life really about? For the first time I questioned success. *If I made $100,000 last year, do I have to make $150,000 this year, and a quarter of a million dollars the year after that? Where does it stop, and when do I consider myself a success?*

As I looked at my boys, still throwing stones into the water, a shocking realization hit me. I said painfully to Sally, "I don't know my own sons." I knew who they were. I knew their names. I knew their pants sizes. I made sure they had food for their tummies, but I didn't really know them as individuals. What exactly was I chasing, anyway? What was it costing us? We returned to civilization disquieted, full of doubts about the path we were traveling.

My successful marketing of insurance polices rewarded me with an all-expense paid trip to Reno, Nevada. Everything that wicked city stood for was against what I had come to believe as a Christian, so I asked the company, "Can I have cash in place of the trip?"

"No."

"Can I have a trip someplace else?"

"No. It's the trip or nothing."

Sally and I looked at the map of Nevada and noticed that south of Reno was a place called Yosemite National Park. "Let's go ahead and take the airline reservations and that hotel room, and let's go to Yosemite each day," I suggested.

Here was a chance for Sally and me to spend some time together. We hired a babysitter and agreed to go. We left Wisconsin for Reno and the MGM Grand Hotel in early August. Later, in Yosemite, we parked and walked up to a crystal-clear stream rushing out of the mountains. It so captivated us that we sat beside it for an hour and a half, just enjoying the song of the water on the rocks. The scent of the pines was strong as we took it into our lungs with each breath. We climbed our first mountains with me wearing patent leather shoes, of all things!

In that quiet setting beside those peaceful streams, climbing those majestic mountains, and in mountain valleys full of pinks and lilies, we heard God speaking to us in a way we had never heard Him speak to us before. After a number of days in this setting, His voice seemed incredibly loud, and He was saying, "Jim and Sally, get off the train."

We realized that not to decide was to decide. Every time God brings us a choice, we make a decision, even if the decision is to do nothing. God had said, "Escape for thy life; look not behind thee . . . Escape to the mountain" (Gen. 19:17 KJV).

## THE PROMISED LAND

We decided on the plane trip home that we were going to try to live the way we felt God was calling us to live. When God created man, He placed him in a garden prepared for him. We couldn't live in the Garden of Eden, but we felt that the closer we could come to God's original plan, the better it would be for our spiritual, mental, and physical health. We decided to follow God's call upon our hearts.

Like Abraham so many years before, we felt like pilgrims following our God to the promised land.

We were determined to put our plans into action. We put the house and the business up for sale. Then we pulled out a map of the United States and planned where we wanted to go. Right away we ruled out some areas. Neither of us likes the hot, humid climate of the South. There were objections to some other areas. The search soon narrowed to three geographical areas: the Upper Peninsula of Michigan, northern Maine, and the Pacific Northwest. We had visited Glacier National Park a few years previously and felt drawn to this gem of the continent.

In September, we visited Montana again and looked extensively over the area surrounding the park. We were concerned that we might locate in an area that would build up around us, forcing us to move again. Finally, on the western edge of the park, we traveled up one of the most beautiful wilderness valleys left in the lower forty-eight states. It was bordered on the east by Glacier National Park and on the west by the Whitefish mountain range.

We noted that the federal government owned 98 percent of the land. It was obvious that even if every piece of private land was developed, the valley could never be overdeveloped. Glancing at each other, we both raised our thumbs up. We had found our valley. We were going to Montana!

The valley runs sixty miles north and south, with a beautiful wild river running down the middle. The population of our valley is 175 people in the entire sixty miles. There was only one forty-acre parcel of land for sale. The real estate agent informed us it had been on the market for five years! This was good news indeed, because we had to sell our house before we could buy anything. If the property hadn't sold for five years, it would probably still be there when we sold our house.

There were not many ways to make a living in this valley, but our plans did not include my working at first anyway. We wanted to use some of the equity from our house to allow me to stay home for the first few years. Sally had been the primary parent in many ways, especially when the boys were very young. Now we both felt they needed more time with their father. We desired to redeem the time.

I was going to take the time I had previously spent running my business and playing or watching sports and invest it in my wife and boys. At last, we were going to have the time to develop a true connection with God.

We were certain that the Lord had led us. We returned to Wisconsin with definite plans for relocation to Montana.

Our plans for relocation may have been taking shape, but our friends and families were adamantly opposed to what we were doing. The very idea struck them as fanatical and foolish.

But we were determined to cut off every influence that hindered a full and complete surrender of ourselves to God. For our children, we would provide the very best environment possible. We would give them the best and guard them from all the rest.

Those who were most opposed were our fellow church members. "Your standard is too high!" they said. "It can't be done!" In a real sense, the world was more approving of what we were setting out to do than were our fellow Christians.

We were not survivalists. We wanted only to cut off the distractions that were preventing us from developing the relationship with God for which we longed. We would eliminate from our lives those things that were good, and beyond that, even those things that were better, so that we could possess that which was best!

Planning to purchase raw land had several consequences, the most important of which was that we had to sell our place by March if we were to get a house built and ready to occupy by the early mountain winter. Any later than this, and even with professional builders, we would be racing the weather. But March came and passed without a nibble on our home, despite much advertising. I couldn't understand what was happening. I knew God had called us, and I felt He had led in our plans, but now I was bewildered. Friends and relatives started to scoff and try to convince us that we had been mistaken. After all, the house hadn't sold by our deadline.

"Lord," I said, "did I misunderstand what You wanted?" At last, I withdrew the house from the market, feeling confused and discouraged.

## SOLD!

In early May, I got a call from a realtor who said, "I saw you had your house on the market a few weeks ago. I have a client who is interested in that type of property. May I bring him to see yours?"

"Certainly you may," I said. He brought a very interested client who spent a considerable period of time with us viewing the property and the equipment I used to maintain it. He wrote us an offer for six thousand dollars over our asking price, so he could purchase the tractor and mowers with the property. When he asked the price of the equipment, I thought he was getting an idea of what it was going to cost when he bought his own. He, however, paid full retail price for them even though they were used.

His reasoning was simple. Mine were nearly new, and the convenience of having them already on the property without his effort was well worth the added expense. Regardless of his reasons, we felt it was an extremely kind gesture, and it lifted our spirits after the long wait to sell our home. Hope sprang anew. Again our plans were set in motion.

The next task was a rummage sale to reduce the excess of our lives—and we had lots of excess! Sally stayed to run the sale while I headed to Montana to buy our place.

Arriving at the Polebridge general store, which has the only public phone for miles around, I called the real estate agent and found the property was still available. "I'm going up there to look at it one more time, and then I'm coming down there to write you an offer for it," I said.

After examining the property again and feeling that it would indeed meet our needs, I returned to the general store and the phone at 2:30.

"I'm sorry," the agent said, "but the property sold at 1:30 this afternoon."

It couldn't be true! In shock and disbelief, I called Sally with the news. Then, disheartened, I went up a little hillside and prayed about the situation. "Jim, get into your car and drive up the valley," the Lord said. Having nothing else to do, I turned northward toward Canada, feeling very sorry for myself.

Toward the upper end of the valley, I found myself pulling into someone's driveway, not even sure why I was doing it. An older man, obviously retired, was outside mowing what would have been grass if there had been any grass. He was instead mowing his weeds. *Well, I'll ask him about properties,* I thought. So I approached him and explained what I was looking for. He immediately said, "Well, I'll sell you my place."

"Is it for sale?" I asked.

"It is now," he replied.

He gave me a tour of the property and the little 960-square-foot log cabin. Slowly it dawned on me: God had a different place picked out for us all along. We bought that little log home on five acres overlooking Glacier National Park and bordering United States Forest Service land. Only later would we realize that the Lord had spared us a home-building project. He was bringing us out to the mountains so we could build our characters rather than a house. We could have gained this same experience in Wisconsin, *if* we hadn't been in debt, which forced me to work long hours and prevented me from gaining any real control over my time. In addition, the influence of family and friends would have made some of our changes harder. When I returned to Wisconsin, the pieces started falling into place. Sally had been busy. She made over ten thousand dollars at our rummage sale. The business sold. The details of the sale would, however, cause us considerable inconvenience in the near future. The purchaser was unable to replace me with another agent until sometime in October. The terms of the sale were that I had to provide at least part-time oversight of the agency until the other agent was in place.

The house closed in early August, and we moved our family to our Montana cabin. I barely had time to begin the settling-in process before I had to return and oversee the business. This left Sally and the boys to continue organizing in the smallest home we had ever owned. This was extremely hard on her, not only because she had to be both mother and father, but also because we were both from a city environment. We had lived in the country, but our lives there were little different from those of thousands of others residing in suburbia. There she was, alone in the wilderness.

I worked like a dog at the agency so I could return to Montana for another two weeks. There, I also worked frantically, not only getting settled but also trying to prepare for the coming winter and getting in a wood supply. So it continued back and forth, one week in Wisconsin, the next two in Montana, driving thirty hours non-stop each way until I was nearing exhaustion.

At last, the new agent was in place, and I made the final drive home to Montana. No one was there! That was baffling, so I went down the road to the home of some people we had befriended to see if they knew anything. Indeed they did! They were caring for my two sons. My wife, they informed me, had crashed from the stress and was in town at the doctor's with pneumonia. It would take three months for her to fully recover.

At last, we were together as a family in our wilderness log cabin. After paying off all our debts and paying cash for the cabin, we had eighteen thousand dollars left over. We divided it into three parts and decided that we would try to live on six thousand dollars a year. This might have been impossible in the suburban environment we'd just left, but there in the wilderness, we felt we might be able to make it on five hundred dollars a month. We were determined to make a go of it.

Our cabin was paid for, and the taxes were less than five hundred a year. Our water came from the creek, and wood supplied heat and hot water, requiring only my labor to cut it. Only the propane generator, which supplied us with electricity, required an expenditure of funds. We used it sparingly to run loads of wash and keep the batteries that powered our home charged. Our utilities were usually less than forty dollars a month.

We lived simply, without things like paper towels and Kleenex, even without many things people might consider essential, such as insurance on our home or health. We couldn't afford such luxuries. We ate simply and cut trees in the forest to supply beams and boards to build a greenhouse in order to grow more of our food.

## TROUBLE

Then it happened! The stress I had been living under for months took its toll. Like Sally, I came down with pneumonia and was very sick. For a month, I was so weak I could hardly get up. Next Sally broke her foot in three places, and we had additional medical expenses.

We pumped the water for the house from the creek, but the weather became extraordinarily cold, and the creek froze all the way to the bottom. We had two small children and no water except what we could melt from snow. Without water we had to use the outhouse rather than the septic system, and without the constant influx of water and organic waste to decompose, our septic system froze up too. We couldn't even put what little water we melted down the drain.

Our truck broke down. Sally fractured her foot a second time and then broke a finger on the neighbor's wringer washing machine. We filled the five-hundred-gallon propane tank used to fuel our generator only to have a bad valve blow out a week later.

We lost all our propane at a time when we could least afford it.

Why was this happening? Was God still with us? We had moved out to the mountains to find God, and we had nothing but trouble and problems from the very beginning. We wondered, as any reasonable person would, who was causing all these problems.

We came to see that God sometimes allows troubles to come to us for character development, and at other times He allows Satan to test and prove us as He did with Job in the Bible. We also realized that people can bring trouble upon themselves with their own ill-considered actions. We prayerfully considered our course and concluded that God had led us, and we had sincerely followed as best we knew. We had not been rebellious, nor had we gone off on our own.

It gradually dawned on us that Satan was trying to discourage us and get us to move back to civilization, where water doesn't freeze up, doctors are close by, and conveniences abound. We came to see that in all these troubles was a message for us. If Satan was that concerned about us moving out there, then we must be on the right track.

The whole family took on the attitude that Satan would try to destroy us, but that if we were faithful, God would sustain us. Slowly, that first winter passed. Finally, spring arrived and with it, the restoration of our water supply. We had been hauling laundry to town, so Sally was eager to wash some clothes at home. We didn't know the septic system was still frozen, and water poured all over the place. Hardships had become such a way of life that Sally and the boys were laughing as they moved bags of grain and other valuables out of reach of the water and started to clean up.

It took time, but we eventually became wilderness wise and learned to prevent water lines from freezing and to stock sufficient wood for the winter.

## IT'S WORTH IT

Our wilderness life didn't save us, my friends. It wasn't a magic cure. If you had watched us in those first years, you would have seen a family struggling to control itself. We developed a schedule and worked hard at fine-tuning it to meet the needs of our family unit. Sally and I set time aside for us and our marriage, which had been a good one but had suffered a slow erosion process because of my inattention. Our relationship began to improve—not that it was an easy transition. I had a hot German temper and Sally had caught the brunt of my intemperate words many times, so I had a lot of past wrongs to make right, hurt feelings to deal with, and most important, self-control to learn in Christ.

We went about this healing process in a real-life setting where the challenge of living on very little money required the expenditure of a great deal of inventive effort. We had sold off many things before we moved, but we still had excess from our days in Wisconsin. To supplement our meager savings, we sold my old hunting gear, our scuba equipment, bowling balls, guns, even excess toys and stuffed animals. We shopped at Goodwill for clothes, and Sally even cut down my extra underwear to sew underwear for the boys. We found ourselves in a real partnership for survival, and it motivated us to work on our relationship because no one else could understand what we were going through.

We finally had control over our time. With time to think and reflect came the opportunity to draw close to God. God was using wilderness living as a tool to draw us to Him without the distractions of the busy life we had led for all those years. Soon the tools that God had given us—a schedule, no distractions, the stern discipline of a simple life, and the grandeur of His creation—began to yield results in our family.

We were drawn toward God and to each other. If you had known us before and had visited us at this point, you would have seen the beginnings of the harvest of joy we were gathering from the hard choices we had made. You would have said, as we did, "It's worth it!"

A minister's wife recently wrote to us:

When I called you, it was because prior to this I had come to the conviction that I needed to slow down, get on a schedule, and spend a lot more time in prayer and in the Word of God. I realized that my husband was not going to join me in my New Year's resolution. Nevertheless, I needed to be committed alone. I understood the concept of good, better, best. I truly wanted to choose the best.

I have failed so miserably. I feel trapped right now. I have somehow scheduled myself as a Bible class teacher and leader, personal ministries leader for two churches, fund-raising coordinator for two churches, health and temperance leader, community outreach helper, Vacation Bible School leader and teacher for two churches, and newsletter and sometimes bulletin editor.

Add to that the church work bees and the pastoral meetings I attend with my husband every single month. I also need to attend seminars for personal ministries leaders and about six other ministry meetings every year with my husband plus board meetings I must attend because I have all these offices in the respective churches.

As I am writing this, it seems crazy to have this kind of schedule in the light of the sanctification that needs to be done in my own life and keeping up with home duties, in which my

husband does not systematically cooperate. I am also in charge of
the finances of our home and assist him as secretary many times.
What do I quit? Where do I start? My life is a constant chase after
unfinished tasks and upset people.

Our Lord never forces us into hurried or complicated move-
ments. Too many try to bear burdens that their merciful heavenly
Father has not put on them. Tasks He never designed them to perform chase one another wildly. It has taken me a long time to
understand that we do not glorify God when we take so many burdens that we become exhausted, lose self-control, and begin to fret
and scold.

Who placed those burdens on the minister's wife? She just
picked up everyone else's expectations. Hence, she gathered to herself troubles that our loving God had never intended her to bear.

Not long ago, I was speaking at a series of meetings, and a
young woman gave me a note when I finished my sermon. It read:
"Call your sister immediately!" My sister and I hadn't talked in
years. Oh, we spoke, but we hadn't talked, I mean really *talked*, in
years. *Why would she search for me in another state with a message like
this?* I wondered. Within five minutes, I was dialing my sister.

Her husband answered. "Praise God you called! Your sister
wants to talk to you!"

"What's up, Joe?"

"I can't tell you, Jim. I'll let Louise tell you."

Louise was in tears. "Jim, I'm so thankful you called. I just came
from the doctor's office. He told me to make out my last will and
testament. He says I'm a basket case. Can I come and stay with you
a month? I need help!"

"Yes, come, sister."

"You're sure? Don't you want to pray about it? I thought you
prayed about everything first."

"Louise, I have been praying about this for ten years. I don't have to get on my knees any longer. I've watched your life. I've seen what it's been doing to you. This is an answer to my prayers. I'll pick you up at the train station. Come!"

When Louise came, she had bleeding ulcers, precancerous cells, and anemia; she was as close to a complete physical and nervous breakdown as anyone I have ever seen. She was forty-six-years-old, and her hands couldn't stop shaking. Her eyes had that far-away look. I took her up to our little mountain home.

What had happened to my sister? We were raised in the same neighborhood, on the same street, in the same family. But she had gotten caught up in the American—I'm not going to say *dream*—myth. My sister was working fourteen hours a day, six to seven days a week. She had found her dream home. Then she felt she had to fill it with exquisite furnishings. Life started controlling her. It was destroying her. It took her doctor to wake her up!

The modern American dream is a myth, but the myth doesn't exist only in America. It exists all over the world. People are caught up in it, and it is destroying their lives.

I told Louise, "We aren't going to preach at you. We have a different lifestyle from yours. You can participate in anything you want to or feel free to reject anything you want to." Our whole family began to minister to her, and she became one with our family in our daily routine. She had worship with us in the morning and in the evening. She sang with us. She walked with us, ate our diet, played pick-up sticks and dominoes with the boys in the evening, and joined in our family reading time.

My wife, a nurse, ministered to Louise, and her health started to improve. As she slowed down, a desire for God was reborn in her heart. At the end of thirty days, my sister told me, "You know, Jim, I can summarize my stay with your family in three words: less is more."

You see, we had a smaller home than she did. We had fewer

furnishings, less clothing, less in the garage, less of everything the world offers, but we had more of what the world can never give. We had love in our home. We had companionship. We had time for one another. That's why she said, "Less is more." I wish that commentary described every Christian home.

## NEVER BORED

I can almost hear someone saying, "The simple life is hard and dull, Jim." Hard, perhaps, but dull? Right out our back door, we see elk and moose. The mountain lions and wolverines still roam free. The grizzly bear travels unhindered though these last primal forests. One day while hanging clothes on the line, I felt a strong nudge from behind as a huge buck put his nose in my back pocket, looking for the little crackers we sometimes fed them. We had the blessed opportunity to tame a wild bear. She allowed us to pet her and even climbed on the swing set with my boys!

Gaining the friendship of wild creatures is a little bit of heaven! Isn't that better than Disneyland? And when you get close to nature, you get close to nature's God.

My boys were never bored. All we had to do was say yes. "Yes, you can go backpacking, canoeing, and cross-country skiing!" "Yes, you can go mountain climbing and rappelling and track down that moose!" "Yes, you can explore that backwoods!" Yes, yes, yes! "And yes, we will go with you."

Children in other environments are told no, no, no! Rebellion sets in. It is so much better to live where children's choices are limited to choices between acceptable options.

By the way, simplicity is a stern discipline, but this is not a new sort of legalism. We do this with Christ so that we may bring Him into our marriages and families. It is not just some new reform that we all follow, thinking that we are the saved ones because we live the simplest lives in the world. Christ lived a simple life, and He is our example. The quiet simplicity of Christ's first thirty years prepared Him for the three-and-a-half busy years of active ministry. Even then, we read in the Bible of His going off by Himself and communing with His heavenly Father. The simple life prepared the way for ministry, and periods of quiet simplicity sustained His ministry.

What is the Holy Spirit saying to you? Is He saying, "Get off the train?" God promises, "My people will dwell in a peaceful habitation, in secure dwellings, and in quiet resting places" (Isa. 32:18 NKJV).

We need to return and find our rest, to find that connection with God. When we experience that quietness and confidence, we will know that God is with us every second of the day. If we are going to find that living, vital connection with Jesus Christ, we must quiet our lives. We must simplify. "In returning and rest you shall be saved; in quietness and confidence shall be your strength" (Isa. 30:15 NKJV).

Not everyone is called to relocate to the wilderness, but everyone is called to have the wilderness experience with God. You can start right where you are, simplifying your life and making time for God and family. It takes no special skills or significant sums of money to accomplish this—just a determination to possess this experience.

The text from Isaiah 30:15 ends with the sad commentary, "But you would not" (NKJV). Friends, it doesn't have to be said of you. Please don't let it be said of you! You can choose to escape to God and find rest. God's solutions for me were personally and uniquely tailored to meet my needs, and I know He will do the same for you!

# Chapter Four

# A BUNDLE OF CHOICES

*Choose for yourselves this day whom you will serve.*
*Joshua 24:15 NKJV*

OUR EFFORTS AT simplification had yielded wonderful results. We had eradicated the busyness and distractions of life. But this alone was not sufficient to bring me any lasting happiness or peace. I knew the Lord had led us out to the wilderness for the primary purpose of our spiritual development. I had yet to discover a practical application of faith and works that would fully transform my life. I had just bits and pieces, little glimpses that there could be something more than what I had thus far achieved.

As I've said, at first, I thought a life of faith involved just belief in certain theological tenets. While I had studied complex theological concepts for years, my studies had never produced the type of character changes that I desired to have in my life. I was still laboring under the misconception that more knowledge, a more complete understanding, and a more perfectly understood theology were all I needed to produce a transformation in my life.

With this in mind, I purchased five books from five well-known and respected theologians. In the wilderness, I finally had both the time and the inclination to obtain a working knowledge of salvation. Eagerly, I started to read. By the time I finished the last book, confusion, unlike any I had ever known, settled upon me. It was clear that not one of the leading scholars agreed with the others. If they couldn't understand or agree on the gospel, what hope did I have?

I knew in my heart of hearts that the gospel could not be as complicated as man had made it. Common sense told me that the true gospel would save me from those areas of my life in which my willpower had proved useless. That gospel would provide me a power with which to control my feelings, my thoughts, and my passions.

Through the guidance of the Lord, I had made many changes in my life, and yet I still longed for peace with God. I still hoped for full assurance of salvation, but I knew that my life, in spite of all my efforts, was not fully in keeping with His Word. Somehow I knew there was more because I saw people in the Bible who were confident in their salvation, and I wasn't.

Oh, I was willing to make a partial surrender to God—I thought it only fitting that I should do that much. But the more I read and the more I studied, the more I became convinced that what I needed was absolute surrender of everything—withholding nothing. I shrank back from this, fearful of the cost. I truly thought that I might be miserable if I gave up my "right" to indulge in sin. My struggle was how to move from doctrine and partial surrender to full surrender to God.

As I shared earlier, we realized early on that our suburban lives were too complicated, too busy. Only after we were in the wilderness did it begin to dawn on me that my theology was suffering from exactly the same problems that had so plagued our life in civilization. It was time, once again, to simplify.

I went back to the Bible with prayerful study. This time I didn't go to prove some theological position or to gain some doctrinal understanding. I went to the Word of God as a sinner in need of salvation. I knew that unless I found a better, deeper, living experience capable of saving Jim Hohnberger from himself, I was lost! When I approached the Bible with that humble and teachable spirit, it became a living fountain speaking not just of truth and error, not just of history or theological concepts, but speaking to the deepest needs of my soul.

I learned that faith is not just an intellectual belief in truth but a willing decision to die to my ideas, wisdom, and desires, surrendering to God and then abiding in Christ, His wisdom guiding me, His Spirit teaching me, and His strength empowering me to do that which He instructs.

I had lived my whole life in a legalistic frame of reference where if you do this, that, and the other thing, then you will be saved. There was nothing wrong with any of the things I was trying to do, but once I gained a working understanding of faith and grace, I at last entered into a new life in Christ and found that what I was actuated to do by love was far easier than that which I used to try to do out of duty. This understanding changed the way I related to the Bible.

When Paul had first explained it, the old Book had come alive, but now from its pages flowed a gospel message that was just as simple and had just as practical an application to my life as did the wilderness lifestyle that God had called us to live. Now the Bible became a living message from God personally to me!

The Bible taught me a gospel message, which in its simplest form is about choices—simple, straightforward, everyday choices. Those choices, when combined, compose the whole length and breadth of the Christian experience. It is my privilege in this chapter to share with you these choices that have so transformed my life.

Some may complain I am oversimplifying the gospel. I truly do not believe this is possible. The gospel should be presented so simply that little children can understand it.

Others may accuse me of teaching salvation by works. Nothing could be further from the truth! Prior to discovering the true gospel, I spent my entire "Christian" life attempting to be good, to change myself, in my own human strength. Surely I understand the futility of such an experience. Yet, I am unashamed of the gospel of Christ that not only can but will produce changes in the life of any man, woman, or child who accepts it. These changes are the inevitable fruit of the gospel.

Those who object to the idea that the Christian can truly obey and do good works have never tasted grace and experienced a power outside of themselves. This power "is able to keep you from falling, and to present you faultless before the presence of his glory with exceeding joy" (Jude 24 KJV).

So if you are inclined to be a critic, you may not look with favor upon the following pages. But if you, like me, long for something better than that which you have experienced; if you want full assurance of salvation, not just theological mumbo jumbo; if you desire peace with God and the resulting peace within yourself; then turn these pages and explore with me this bundle of choices.

## A MORMON BUSINESSMAN

A newly married man and his wife started it all. As they sat in the departure lounge of the Salt Lake City Airport waiting for their flight, they visited quietly over the open Bible in his lap. The man was a recently ordained evangelical minister, and his earnestness and zeal were unmistakable. They were a hard couple not to notice, so obviously in love, and yet it was that open Bible that set them apart from the average traveler.

Al, a devout Mormon businessman, noticed it too. He sat

across from them as he waited for the same flight. He observed the pair as discreetly as possible, averting his eyes if they glanced in his direction. Al was a very proper man and would never have wanted to be so rude as to stare at someone. Too late he realized that the young couple had been aware of his interest in them for some time.

Suddenly the Bible shut as the young man stood and strode purposefully to this stranger whose attention they had so clearly captivated.

Al had visited my family a few short months before. He was a successful businessman in western Montana, not far from where we live. He came to our home with two young Mormon missionaries. I assume the purpose of their visit was to enlighten me about Mormonism, but God appeared to have other plans.

Al became so enthralled as he learned of our lifestyle, our goals for country living, and our understanding of the gospel that he and I drew close together as we visited, forming the beginnings of a lasting friendship. Meanwhile the two missionaries were quiet and uncomfortable, hardly saying a word while Al undermined the very reason for their visit with his interest in our faith. I found Al to be a fascinating man, an independent thinker who was unafraid to examine his own beliefs and values. This rare trait endeared him to me, and I was determined to keep in touch with him whenever possible.

Traveling near Al's office one day, I decided to visit him. He was genuinely glad to see me, and after we had exchanged greetings, he told me of his experience in the airport:

"Excuse me, sir," the young minister had said as he approached Al. "I couldn't help noticing your glances in our direction. May I ask you a question?"

"Certainly," Al responded, while inwardly chiding himself for disturbing the quiet young couple.

"Sir, if our flight were to crash before we reached our destination and all of us were to die, would you be sure of eternal salvation?"

"I think I would," my friend replied.

"That's not good enough," said the earnest young man. "You must know! Now let me ask you again. If you were to die today, would you be saved?"

"I don't know" was Al's honest response.

"Listen," said the minister. As he flipped through the pages of his Bible, he read John 3:16: "For God so loved the world that He gave His only begotten Son, that whoever believes in Him should not perish but have everlasting life" (NKJV); then John 6:47: "Most assuredly, I say to you, he who believes in Me has everlasting life" (NKJV); and finally, John 11:25: "I am the resurrection and the life. He who believes in Me, though he may die, he shall live" (NKJV).

"There," he said triumphantly. "Now, if you were to die today, would you be saved?"

"Yes, I believe so," Al said.

"Then," said the young minister, becoming animated, "you are a Christian, and you have eternal life."

"You know," Al said to the young man, "I really admire your enthusiasm. I used to have that kind of zeal when I went out on my missions."

"Missions!" the young man squawked. "You used to go out on missions! Why, are you a Mormon?" he asked distastefully.

"Yes," Al said, bewildered at the sudden change.

"Why didn't you say you were a Mormon?"

"You never asked."

"Well, I'm sorry," said the minister, "but Mormons won't be in heaven." With those parting words, he turned and walked away.

As he finished his story, Al slowly turned to me and said, "Jim, I'm confused. Can you shed some light on this subject?"

"I'll try," I responded. It was clear Al wasn't concerned about the unfair and prejudiced treatment he had received. He was intelligent enough to ignore the irrelevancy of the young man's bias. Al was struggling with the deeper issue of how to know, really know, whether he was saved or lost.

*Lord,* I prayed in my thoughts, *give me the wisdom and the words to satisfy this man. Help me to reach across the barriers we place between each other because of denominational affiliation, doctrinal bias, or misunderstandings.*

"Al, the Christian life is not made up of doctrines, creeds, reforms, or church membership. It is not even made up of beliefs, but rather the Christian life is a bundle of choices. When God brings a truth or light to our understanding, it always comes with a choice. We must choose to submit to the will of God or refuse. When God has all my known choices, then He has me.

"Let's say for purposes of illustration that the Christian life in its entirety is made up of a hundred choices. Remember the thief on the cross?" I asked.

He nodded, so I continued. "Well, that thief didn't know a whole lot about the Christian life. His mind may have been aware of only a handful of the choices that compose the Christian life— let's say perhaps ten. But for those ten choices that he knew of, he was fully submitted to God. Christ could offer him full assurance of salvation not because of his great knowledge, but because he chose to surrender to God in *all* his known choices. Had he lived longer, he would have had opportunity to have advanced in his Christian experience, and his choices would have deepened and broadened to encompass the whole gamut of the Christian life.

"Then there was Caiaphas, the Jewish high priest who wanted Jesus killed. He was aware of many truths in God's Word. He had lots of light, and that gave him, maybe, seventy choices. Yet, let's say that he made a freewill choice to submit to God in only fifty of those choices. He had more choices, was surrendered in more of his choices than the thief, yet despite his greater knowledge and additional choices, he was in rebellion to God. If he had been on the cross instead of the thief, Jesus couldn't have given him full assurance of salvation. Why? He had not submitted all his known choices and surrendered his will completely to God. The thief had.

"Al," I said, "do you believe that Jesus came to earth and as your Substitute paid the price for your sins?"

"Yes, I do."

"Do you love the Lord with all of your heart and mind and soul?"

"Yes, I do."

"Then," I said, "you have accepted Jesus as your Substitute. That is good, but it is not in and of itself complete. You must have Jesus as Lord of your life. Are you, at this moment, fully in submission to all your known choices? Are you at peace with God?"

"No, I'm not," Al answered quietly.

"Then you have not accepted Christ as your Lord, and without accepting Him as Lord, your desire to have Him as your Savior is not sufficient to bring you either peace with God in this present life, or salvation in the life to come. For these two are inseparably one!

"Al, all of us are a work in process. Sometimes we answer the call of God for our hearts' surrender, and God can take us deeper; other times we resist. All of us are human in that we stumble and fall, but some of us get up and continue going deeper with Christ, as Peter did, while others become entrenched in their rebellion, like Judas.

"But, Al, let a man, any man, stubbornly and persistently resist in even just one area and this resistance will eventually lead him to join in the great revolt against God started by Satan himself. No matter how much we may desire Jesus to be our Savior, no matter how much we feel our hearts are drawn out in love toward Him, determined resistance to His leadership will, in the end, destroy us, just as it did Lucifer.

"The key is not that we are perfect but that we are perfectly surrendered to God in all that we know He is calling us to. It is not the individual act, sin, or misdeed that compromises salvation although every such act is sin and needs confession and forgiveness. These are not indicative of a permanent decision to resist God. It is the attitude of the heart and mind, the stubborn and settled unwillingness to yield to God that eventually unfits us for His kingdom."

"I see, Jim. I've never understood this before," Al said, obviously struggling to come to terms with this new understanding. "Thank you."

## CHOICES

My conversation with Al ended there, but there is more in that Bible story that we could understand. Two other men made choices we can learn from that same day. The first was Peter. He had followed Jesus for most of His active ministry. He had great opportunity and had been exposed to great light. Though just a simple fisherman, he may have had, through his exposure to Jesus, as many known choices as the high priest. And Peter was in submission to God on most of them.

In a few small areas, however, he would not submit. He had not surrendered to God his desire for self-exaltation, his cultivated national pride, and his stubborn self-assurance, and soon he found himself denying that he even knew Jesus. He was Christ's own disciple, and he failed because he had not submitted all his known choices.

Jesus is the other man who was faced with choices that day. Jesus demonstrated only surrender and submission to His Father's will in His choices, but the struggle is evident in His pleas to His Father in Gethsemane: "O My Father, if this cup cannot pass away from Me unless I drink it, Your will be done" (Matt. 26:42 NKJV).

He had to choose just as we do. If we will adopt Jesus' attitude of "not my will, but Yours be done," it will lead us to choose correctly even when we don't feel like it.

It is at this point that many are confused and finding difficulties in living the Christian life, for becoming a Christian is not a onetime choice but rather a minute-by-minute, continuous choice to let God have all of us.

Day in and day out, I am to live for Jesus. My focus is to be on His will, His way. Many attempt to accomplish this through their own humanity. They set out with their strong willpower and their teeth gritted in determination to live the Christian life. It always ends in defeat.

How then is it possible to live every day, every hour, every moment to the glory of God? It's very simple. We are to live as Jesus did. Mark 1:35 states, "Now in the morning, having risen a long while before daylight, He went out and departed to a solitary place; and there He prayed" (NKJV). I believe this was something Jesus did every morning. I believe this because He depended upon His Father. He even said, "Most assuredly, I say to you, the Son can do nothing of Himself . . . I can of Myself do nothing. As I hear, I judge; and My judgment is righteous, because I do not seek My own will but the will of the Father who sent Me" (John 5:19, 30 NKJV). Jesus was God incarnate and aware of His power, but He chose to live a life on earth as we do, thereby demonstrating for us the way of salvation. Hence, Jesus took time with God every morning.

We, too, must take time to give ourselves to God every morning, to surrender at the beginning of every day. It can't be a rushed thing; we have to allow time to commune with God and really listen to what He's saying to us individually. God speaks to us through the Bible, nature, providence, and impressions on the mind. After communing with our Father and making sure there is nothing to prevent us from hearing His voice, we can rest assured that He will guide us throughout the rest of the day.

When we leave our place of quiet devotion, it is essential that we take God with us in order to continually commune with Him.

We need to learn to ask, "Lord, what do You want me to do?" (Acts 9:6 NKJV). God wants us to know we are not in this alone. We need help from a source outside of ourselves at the beginning of the day and then all through the day. As we learn to be sensitive to the Holy Spirit's promptings upon our hearts and learn to submit our wills to always do His will, then it is that "Christ lives in me" (Gal. 2:20 NKJV).

But then temptation comes—perhaps the very same temptation that we have often yielded to before. In the past, we have gritted our teeth and tried to resist the temptation until we either failed or forced ourselves to obey. There is no peace or joy in such an experience.

Friends, the true conflict of temptation occurs in the heart. I first must decide if I want to remain surrendered to God. When surrender is my choice, self dies and the victory is won, and then God supplies all the power to meet the temptation.

This experience is hard because self must die, but it is the only path to peace and joy as a Christian!

Now, choice doesn't merit me anything with God. I am not saved by my choices. The very desire to make the choice of submission to God is a gift from His grace. Salvation is fully the gift of God, yet it is that choice to submit that allows God the freedom to transform our lives through the ministry of His grace upon the human heart.

It is vitally important to see this, for most who have taken the name of Christ live a strange amalgamation of Christ and self, contending for the management of the life. This type of Christian life is like a yo-yo, continuously up and down. Being born of the Spirit is going from this experience to allowing Christ to be the sole Ruler of the life. When this amalgamation ends, there is rest for the soul. Then we learn the true science of salvation and the language of heaven, which is simply how to allow Christ full access to all our decisions and then by His grace, through a living faith, to say yes to God and no to self.

Every choice we face offers an opportunity for us to choose to surrender our will and way to God. The Bible speaks of this as a death to self. Christ illustrated it this way: "Unless a grain of wheat falls into the ground and dies, it remains alone; but if it dies, it produces much grain" (John 12:24 NKJV).

How is wheat grown? It must be buried in the grave, so to speak, and for the rest of the plant's life, it draws its strength from this grave. Christians must live in the same manner, rooted in Calvary, not merely giving an assent to Calvary, but truly entering into a Calvary experience.

No, we cannot die *for* sin as Christ did, but we can die *to* sin. As I've mentioned, Paul wrote about this in Galatians 2:20: "I have been crucified with Christ; it is no longer I who live, but Christ lives in me; and the life which I now live in the flesh I live by faith in the Son of God" (NKJV).

Paul also said, "I die daily" (1 Cor. 15:31 NKJV). Obviously Paul did not literally die daily; he referred to the true Christian experience where we must die to self daily. He encouraged us to "reckon yourselves to be dead indeed to sin, but alive to God in Christ Jesus our Lord" (Rom. 6:11 NKJV).

The choice of putting self to death and submitting to God's will is well illustrated in Scripture. Perhaps 2 Corinthians 4:11 says it best: "For we who live are always delivered to death for Jesus' sake, that the life of Jesus also may be manifested in our mortal flesh" (NKJV). This is true Christianity. Let me illustrate.

## "I Don't Like This, Lord!"

One cold winter morning not long ago, I awoke at my normal time and spent more than two hours in Bible study and prayer. I seek after God in the morning, knowing my own weakness and realizing that yesterday's experience will not save me from today's trials. Every morning just before breakfast time, we gather to worship God as a family and to ask His guidance and protection throughout the day. It is a special time for our family that draws us together in strong bonds of love, which last throughout the day.

After our family worship time, I looked out the window on the beautiful sight of sixteen new inches of white, fluffy snow. My wife was making waffles, and I could see the blueberry sauce bubbling on the stove. Now, I love waffles, and adding the blueberry sauce is just like icing on the cake. With one of my favorite breakfast meals underway, I decided to take a few minutes while the waffles were cooking and plow the driveway.

We get a lot of snow in the mountain valley where I live, many, many feet of it each winter, and there are several ways we can remove that snow. I can use a snow shovel—the hard way—or I can use our large snow blower—better—but shortly after moving to the wilderness, I decided I needed a plow to fit on my Toyota Land Cruiser.

You will remember that we were living on a very small income, and a three-thousand-dollar Western plow with hydraulic lift was totally out of the budget. However, using a little ingenuity and investing about sixty dollars in some lumber, I built a V-shaped plow out of trusses and covered it with tin. I attached this to the front of my bumper, and it free-floated over the road, clearing the snow and saving me huge amounts of time.

I was very pleased with my homemade plow, and while it wasn't necessarily beautiful, the effort it saved me was beautiful. Traveling down my driveway with the snow flowing off the plow to each side, I was enjoying the Christmas-card scenery and having a great day with the Lord.

My driveway is a third of a mile long, and, toward the end, I could see that the huge county snowplow had left a great big berm of snow. I sensed the still, small voice of God warning me that I should not try and fight my way through, but I reasoned it away.

After all, I had plowed through piles of snow before. The plow rode up over the berm, then dropped down toward the road surface. In the meantime, while the plow was dropping downward, my vehicle was driving up over that big pile of snow. So when the front end of the vehicle started to drop back down toward the road, it lodged firmly on top of the plow, the front of the truck in the air. The front tires were useless.

My four-wheel-drive vehicle was stranded. I was stuck with my truck blocking the road. I began to get concerned because where I live there is a long, blind curve, and anybody coming up that way could easily hit me without ever having a chance to stop. Just as this anxiety began to rise in my flesh, the Lord called for my heart. "Jim, surrender it to Me," that still, small voice said.

I had chosen that morning to surrender all my choices to Him. Now I had to renew that choice, and even though I hate inconveniences, I chose to give Him my thoughts and feelings. Then I quickly added, "Lord, I am in a dangerous position here. I know our road gets very little traffic, but please don't let me get hit out here."

There was only one thing to do. I was going to have to get under the vehicle and jack up the front end. Thankfully, the front of my truck rested on the plowed surface of the Northfork Road, providing me a firm surface on which to rest the jack. This would enable me to disconnect the plow and pull it out of the way. With the plow out of the way, I could lower the vehicle to the ground, then reattach the plow.

Crawling under the front end, I found myself immediately facing a new frustration and temptation to let go of Jesus and give vent to my feelings. You see, when you are plowing fluffy, white snow and then crawl under a hot engine, all the snow that has been kicked up on the undercarriage melts. I felt as if I were in a shower. It was dripping down my exposed face and neck. As if this weren't bad enough, the drops fell in my eyes, which would have been irritating even with clean snowmelt, but this melt carried with it all the grime of the undercarriage.

Immediately I wanted to feel sorry for myself. I was so tempted to say, *Poor me,* and have a pity party.

"Yield it to Me," God called in His quiet voice.

"But Lord," I responded, "I don't like this!"

"Jim, it is not a question of whether you like this or not. It is a question of your willingness to surrender even these irritations to Me." You see, self-surrender is the substance of the teachings of Christ. I was still learning this hard lesson.

"OK, Lord, You can have these circumstances," I responded. "Just don't let me get hit here in the middle of the road."

Almost instantly, I could hear another vehicle coming down the road. *Oh no!* As I rushed to extricate myself from under the truck, I struck my head on the back of the engine. It was a nice hard whack, the kind that raises a lump on your skull. "Lord," I said, "this just isn't fair, and I don't like it!"

"Surrender those feelings to Me, Jim. Don't yield to them. I'm with you."

Once again, I had to choose, and once again, through the grace of God, I submitted to God and gained the victory over my thoughts and feelings. Faith is not only belief in God but also a surrender of all my choices to Him, daily, hourly, moment by moment.

Looking over at the vehicle on the road, I noticed it had stopped, and two men, trappers, got out. They came over to investigate. They looked at my plow and the mess I was in with amusement. They hadn't even said hello, and they were making fun of my plow. I wanted to straighten them out, but the Lord spoke to me again and asked me to surrender the irritation to Him.

"Why don't you get a real plow?" one of the men said.

I could just feel the anger rising in me. My flesh wanted to fight back, and again Jesus called to me to surrender it. By His grace through faith, I made the choice to surrender those feelings to Him. The gospel is quite simple. It's just a matter of saying yes to God and no to self. That's a faith that works.

"Look," I said, "I'm in quite a fix here. Do you fellows think you could hook up a chain to the front of the plow and use your truck to pull it out from under me? That way I can hook it back up in just a minute and get out of the middle of the road, so you guys can continue on your way."

They consented to do this, and within minutes I was back in business. I thanked them, and they drove away. My youngest son, Andrew, came down the driveway at that point. My wife knew how long it should have taken to plow the drive, so she figured there must have been a problem and sent him to check on me.

Seeing that I was OK, he asked, "What happened?"

"It's a long story," I told him.

"Well, as long as you're all right," Andrew said, "I am going down to the neighbors'. They're away, and I promised to feed Odie for them."

I felt as though I had just fought a war and won. It was only nine o'clock in the morning, and I was exhausted. In the past, any one of those inconveniences would have been enough to make me let go of Jesus and give way to self. Sadly, I could recall, all too well, that when I let go and gave in to the frustrations, I took it out on my wife and family. I was grumpy with them as if it were their fault. You see, that's what sin does in our lives. It makes us, and everyone around us, unhappy.

"Andrew," I said, "why don't you hop in, and I'll drive you down there? You can feed the dog, and I will plow out their drive. That way, when they get home, they will be pleased that they don't have to dig out themselves."

"Great!" said Andrew, and down the road we went to the

neighbors'. I had plowed most of the way to the house when I came upon four trees that had fallen over the driveway in the snow.

*I am stuck!* I couldn't back up their drive because of the home-made plow, and I couldn't continue forward. I felt as if I should never have gotten out of bed that morning. Again I had to choose to submit my feelings and thoughts to God. It is only by a constant renunciation of self and a continuous dependence on Christ that we can live the Christian life.

"Andrew," I said at last, "go ahead and feed their dog, and I will get on the radio and ask Mother to send Matthew down here with the chain saw. We can remove these trees and be on our way home." So, off he went to the house. Sally promised to send Matthew right down, and I got out of the truck to look the situation over, only to glance down and see that I had a flat tire.

"No, Lord. This is just too much. I don't want to have a flat tire!" I wailed.

"You don't have to let go, Jim. You can choose to hold on if you want to."

"All right, Lord. I will submit this to You. But I'm getting tired, Lord." I got out the jack and proceeded to change the tire, by which time Andrew was back.

"Odie won't let me in the door!" he exclaimed.

I wanted to get upset, and again I felt the constraint of the Lord to keep quiet and speak gently to my son. Matthew should have been there by now, but he was nowhere in sight, and once more the flesh wanted to rise and think all manner of evil about my son.

"Jim," God's still, small voice spoke in the quiet of my mind, "yield those thoughts to Me. You have held on this far. Don't give up now. I will never leave you nor forsake you. Please don't forsake Me, Jim."

"OK, Lord. I'll just go and look for him."

Starting out to see what had become of Matthew, we had barely climbed up the drive before he came panting down, hauling the chain saw. What struck me most was that he had obviously been working hard. He was perspiring and covered in sawdust and wood chips from the chain saw.

"Father, I have been cutting down the trees leaning over our driveway and—"

"Never mind, son." I said. "We'll talk about it later." There was no way I could trust myself to speak to my son. The promptings of the Lord were clear. Besides, it mattered not where the communication had broken down; the chain saw was there now, and I could almost taste the waffles.

"Matthew," I said, "you drive the truck, and I will go in front of you and saw those trees out of the way." Shortly thereafter, the last tree was removed.

I told the boys, "Listen, I'm going to clear the area by their garage. Matthew, you go down to the house with your brother and help him feed that dog. Odie knows you real well. I'm sure he'll let you in."

As I finished the last couple of swipes in front of the garage, I could see the boys were having problems. "He's not letting us in," Matthew said.

The temptation to complain about my boys immediately rose up, and I wanted to say, "Can't you guys do anything by yourselves?" Thankfully, the Lord had not left me. He was still there, pleading for my heart. The devil was saying, "Let go! Go ahead and let go!" God was there too. He was whispering to me, "Hang on, Jim! Hang on to Me. You don't have to let go of Me and say words you'll regret." None of us have to let go. It's always a matter of choice.

"Listen, boys," I said. "I'm going to grab hold of that dog, and when I do, you run in there as fast as you can and put down that food and water. Then we will go home and have breakfast. I'm hungry!" Then silently I added, "Lord, please don't let that dog bite me! That would just be too much!"

Odie is not a little toy poodle. He is an Alaskan elkhound and just as big and tough as the name of his breed. I grabbed the dog and got him in a headlock. He was growling and snuffing and fighting for all he was worth. My boys never moved so fast as they fed and watered that dog. They were out of the house in short order. As soon as I let go, Odie ran over to his bowl and started to eat. I shut the door and climbed wearily into the driver's seat.

"You're doing great, Father!" my boys encouraged me. No one knows us, or the struggles we go through, the way our families do. My boys knew that their father would normally have been in real trouble with only a fraction of the problems we had faced this morning.

"Well, praise the Lord," I managed to say weakly. "But I'm getting tired. I feel as if I fought World War I, World War II, and the Vietnam War all by myself this morning. Thank God it's over, all over."

Amos 5:19 tells of a man who had lots of trouble. He was fleeing from a lion when he ran into a bear. Finally he got into a house and leaned his hand on the wall only to have a serpent bite him. That's the kind of morning I was having. I had been running from the lion and had evaded the bear, and guess who was waiting for me at home?

That's right—the serpent. There never is a time when the Christian can say, "It's all over." That's just when the devil loves to kick us, knowing we are tired and starting to relax. The words "Thank God it's over" were hardly out of my mouth when the bottom of my plow fell off, stopping me almost within sight of the house. "Lord," I breathed to myself, "this is not fair! I'm very tired. I can almost smell the waffles and now another problem."

"You're right, Jim. The trials you are having this morning are not fair, and it was not fair that I should have to leave heaven to die for your sins. Jim, fairness has nothing to do with the situation. You have a choice! This may be unfair, but you can still surrender it to Me and gain the victory."

"Very well, Lord," I said, "You can have it." I went to the garage to get a hammer and some nails. Andrew got out the snowblower to clean the area around the garage, and Matthew went in to help his mother. I continued to wrestle with the plow. I had placed a false bottom on the plow to keep snow from accumulating inside it and weighing it down. Now I nailed it back in place and pulled up to the house.

As I approached the garage, I could see Andrew pushing our snowblower around the corner. You don't push a snowblower! They are self-propelled. This could only mean one thing. It was broken!

*No!* I just couldn't take another problem. I felt tired and weak. My blood sugar was down. I was shaky, and as I walked toward Andrew, I could hear God calling to my heart, calling for me to surrender. Instead, I chose to vent! I gave way to irritation. I blurted out in harshness and anger, *"Who did it?"*

Andrew stopped dead in his tracks and said nothing. Matthew and Sally had come out to the porch to call us in to eat, and there I was. Everyone had seen and heard what had happened. I lifted up the snowblower and dropped down on my knees to look for the problem. I could hear God calling to my heart. "Come back, Jim. Make things right!"

But I wasn't sure I wanted to. Looking at the snowblower, I could see that a little setscrew that held the gears in contact with the driveshaft was missing. We live in the wilderness, and it is a three-hour round-trip to town to get a new setscrew. Closing my eyes, I said, "Lord, if there is any mercy, please be merciful to me and forgive me."

Opening my eyes, I saw something out of the corner of my eye, a little black speck. Walking over to where it lay, I saw it was the setscrew. The Lord had allowed me to see more than twelve feet away in sixteen inches of fresh snow. What a good God we serve! I replaced the setscrew and joined my family at the table for our belated breakfast.

I had a grin on my face that went almost ear to ear. My family was incredulous! I could easily read their thoughts. *Why are you smiling? You just let go. We all saw you do it!*

"Look," I said to my family, "I know you are wondering why I am so happy, but today I held on to Jesus in more trying circumstances than I have ever held on to Him before. I gained victories over irritation today that I have never gained before. Yes, I know that I failed out there with the snowblower, and yet I didn't wait for a hour or a day or even several days to return to the Lord. I repented right away and asked His forgiveness, and now I ask yours. I'm excited not because I failed, but because I can see the Lord working in my life, and I know that He who has begun a good work in me will finish it!"

Praise God, externals don't need to control us. When we learn to choose Christ as first, last, and best in everything, continually, soon our choices become habit, and habits form our character.

## ON THE WRONG SIDE OF THE ROAD

My family was privileged once to spend a month on the island of St. Croix. This island, a former British possession, retains several customs from the United Kingdom. The one we noticed most was driving on the left, or the "wrong" side of the road, as we view it. After obtaining a rental car from the airport, I pulled over and told the whole family that they were going to help me drive this car because absolutely everything was on the wrong side. It was the most awkward experience I can recall. I had to force myself not to revert to old driving habits.

Amazingly enough, after thirty days, I found that I could drive about without even thinking about overcoming the old habits. I had retrained myself and it had become as easy to drive this new way as it had been to drive the old. On our return to the United States, we wondered whether we would have the same kind of adjustment back to the old ways. There was no transition at all. We could still drive just the same as we always had.

Here was a lesson we could readily apply to the Christian walk. It is hard for us to change the manner in which we have always responded to God, and many who start to walk with God find it so awkward and so crucifying to their self-will that they are inclined to quit. Yet if they persevere, they will find it becomes easier and easier to submit.

Still, just as we found we could still drive in the U.S., so will the Christian find that he can still choose at any time to go back to the old life of sin. Choice is precious to God, and He never takes the power to choose away from any of His children. He has instead given us a bundle of choices. Those choices determine our eternal destiny as well as our present happiness. Escaping to God is simply returning all our choices to Him continually until habit becomes character and we are fully His!

*Chapter Five*

# WHERE YOU ARE—GOD IS

Surely the LORD is in this place, and I did not know it.
*Genesis 28:16 NKJV*

Lo, I am with you alway, even unto the end of the world.
*Matthew 28:20 KJV*

IT SEEMS THAT this is exactly where we ended up: Polebridge, Montana, the end of the world. Fifty miles separate us from the nearest paved road or electric utilities. Things most of us take for granted in civilization, such as running water, require expenditures of energy and inventiveness. We have no thermostat to crank up for more heat. Instead, we have to put more wood on the fire.

Living in the wilderness has made us acutely aware of the effort involved in all the modern technology we take for granted. Here we learned that nothing happens automatically and that every little benefit we once enjoyed came as a result of careful planning and hard work.

People who visit our home today do not realize what a rough, basic structure it was years ago, without many of the time-saving additions we've made, such as gravity-flow water and an improved electrical system. In the old days, we got water from a pump in the creek, and it was an endless source of aggravation when it didn't work just right. Now when we run our computers or turn on the lights, our cabin seems like any other house—unless you understand, as we do, the simple magic that turns on the lightbulb.

With no power company available, we depend on a generator. Not the kind homeowners use for power outages or contractors use when they're doing a job, but a heavy-duty propane machine of the type used to supply emergency power to hospitals, albeit smaller. Even a heavy-duty machine can't run continually, so we use the generator to charge banks of batteries, and those batteries supply us with power even when the generator is turned off.

When we first moved up to the wilderness, we couldn't afford to run the generator very much. We used it just to power hungry devices such as the washing machine.

If there is no power, I can't call the power company—I am the power company! In like manner, I am responsible for all other services Sally and I enjoy. If this sounds like a lot of work, you are correct, but it is also freedom and security from external service problems. Nowadays, I have years' worth of wood cut and stored, but this all had to come from somewhere; I spent many, many hours in those early wilderness years building up a supply.

Our beloved home is located but a few short miles from the Canadian border. Due to the relatively scarce population of our wilderness valley, an accident or injury can be a serious, life-threatening situation. No one may be passing by for a long time, perhaps hours, maybe days. Thus, our reliance is ever upon our divine Companion. He never leaves us alone!

## SPRING-LOADED!

Fall in the mountains is a beautiful season of crisp days and fantastic colors. One particular fall day found my wife homeschooling the boys while I headed out to cut some firewood. Hard experience gathering wood in the snow that first winter had been a good teacher. I was determined not only to obtain sufficient firewood for the coming winter but to work toward my long-range goal of always maintaining two years' worth of wood on hand. I wanted to be prepared in the event that I was injured or sick and couldn't do hard physical labor. A two-year supply would give me sufficient reserves to avert a crisis.

Up the valley at Teepee Lake, I pulled off the road in an area where I had noticed some standing deadwood earlier in the season. As I parked my vehicle, I saw up on a little ridge, not more than thirty feet high, a tree had fallen and was wedged between two other trees. It was about eighteen inches in diameter, gray, clearly dead and dry, so I made a mental note to save room for that tree and proceeded to cut the other trees I had planned to take.

Climbing up the little ridge, I stood on the downhill side of the tree and started working from the top of the tree toward its base, cutting sixteen-inch sections of log for my woodstove. As each section of log fell to the ground, I gently pushed it with my heel off the edge of the ridge to roll down the steep incline. The logs came to rest near my vehicle.

This was a great system, and while it required me to stand at the edge of the drop-off, there was sufficient room to complete the operation, so I never gave the process a second thought. As I reached the section that was wedged between the trees and began to make the cut that would free the trunk, I sensed that I should move to the other side of the tree. I reasoned it away. After all, my system of cutting off the sections had worked perfectly.

That morning, however, I had asked the Lord to guide and

direct me. I desired Him to be my constant Companion and had told the Lord that when He impressed me to do something, I would obey. The impression came again, and this time I paused. "Lord, is that You? Are You asking me to move to the other side?"

"Yes, Jim," came the distinct reply.

"OK, Lord," I said, changing my position to the other side of the tree, "but this is ridiculous."

Completing the cut I had started on the other side, I stared in astonishment as several hundred pounds of log snapped outward toward the very spot in which I had been standing moments before. I didn't realize that when the tree had fallen, it had wedged in between the other trees with tremendous tension. It had been, in essence, spring-loaded, just waiting for me to free it with that last fatal cut.

I felt weak as I realized what that impact would have felt like had I not moved. That log would have transferred the kinetic energy of its movement into a crushing impact with my legs at about the level of my knees, catapulting me off the edge of that ridge with the chain saw still running in my hands to land some thirty feet below. I probably would have been killed outright by the impact and subsequent fall with the saw. If not, there was little chance I would have survived until someone found me. No one knew exactly where I was.

I understood without a doubt that the Lord had saved me from, at the very least, serious injury, and more likely, death. I was learning that the Lord was there, even in that wilderness valley, ready to help me before I ever realized that I needed help.

Ephesians 2:8 says it this way: "For by grace are ye saved through faith; and that not of yourselves: it is the gift of God" (KJV). Grace is God's continual presence in my life. It woos me, entreats me, and beckons to me, trying to save me from myself. If I will but listen, the Spirit will guide me, empower me, and protect me.

If God does all of that, then what is my part? I must be willing to continually surrender to the Spirit's moving. That's faith! It's a conscious choice to cooperate with His presence. It makes all the difference between being catapulted off the edge of a steep ridge and staying in step with my divine Helper.

## BEARS!

Glacier National Park and the surrounding area hold one of the largest concentrations of grizzly bears found in the lower forty-eight states. Every year brings us stories of bear attacks on the human visitors in the park. Now, bears do not read survey maps. If they did, they would notice that in crossing the river, they leave Glacier National Park and enter the U.S. Forest Service land that borders our property. But man-made boundaries mean nothing to these creatures whose actions are unpredictable at times.

When we moved to the mountains and took up residence next door to these grand animals, we had friends seriously suggest we arm ourselves against the threat these wild creatures posed. I rejected this idea. I couldn't believe that the very same God who had led us this far was going to allow a bear to attack or eat us. Hence, I rested in the knowledge that the Lord would be with us, for it was God's grace that had brought Sally and me to this pristine wilderness valley.

Sally's past hindered her adjustment to our furry neighbors. When she was young, her older brothers had teased her by telling her that a bear lived under her bed and was going to jump out and get her. Until old enough to realize the foolishness of such a concept, she lived in fear that this would really happen. So my dear wife came to the wilderness of Montana with a long-standing and deeply cultivated fear of bears.

The problem was that in Montana, the bears were no mere

objects of childhood fantasy; they were a grim reality as far as Sally was concerned. While these real bears might not jump out at her from under her bed as she had grown up fearing, they could and did step out of the woods without the slightest warning. Only those who have had contact with wild bears can appreciate how quietly such a large animal can move through the woodlands.

It is a hard thing to put away cultivated fears, even harder if those fears have some basis in reality. That's just what Sally had to do, and it was a struggle. She had read that "perfect love casts out fear" (1 John 4:18 NKJV). She also read, "And I, the LORD, will be their God . . . I will make a covenant of peace with them, and cause wild beasts to cease from the land; and they will dwell safely in the wilderness and sleep in the woods" (Ezek. 34:24–25 NKJV).

Still, time and again those old fears rose up as real as ever, and her only escape was to surrender them to God and trust in her faithful Companion. Slowly, she was learning that where God is, fear need not abide. It was an ongoing battle against old habits and inclinations until the day she met her old nemesis face-to-face.

Friends had told us of a mother (sow) bear in our area that had three cubs with her that spring. Triplets are a little more uncommon than twins, so we hoped we would see them. We took our desires to the Lord during family worship one morning; we prayed that the Lord would open up an opportunity for us to see this sow and her cubs. Of course, Sally added, "Safely, Lord."

After worship we noticed a bear cub in a small tree just fifteen or so feet from the window. Sure enough, two more cubs were on the ground with the big sow nearby. As we watched out the window, we could see the sow's nose moving as she analyzed the scents that were reaching her.

"Oh, look," Sally commented, "I bet she smells the waffles cooking." She did! We watched awestruck as the bear dropped down to all fours and ambled toward the porch. It was a warm

spring morning, and the only thing preventing the bear from walking into the house was a thin screen door, which the bear could step
right through if she so desired.

Sally, being very practical, moved quickly to the doorway with
the intention of shutting the heavy inner door. Upon reaching the
doorway, however, Sally saw the bear was not there, so she opened
the screen door to look out and watched as the bear climbed over
the porch railing and onto the porch. Nothing prevented the bear
from just walking politely up the steps to the porch, but climbing
over the rail seemed to suit her better. When you're a bear, few
people question your manners.

Sally had stepped back and allowed the screen door to close,
but she never got around to shutting the inner door. My two boys
and I watched with gaping mouths as she stood in the doorway
while the bear came right up to the door. Sally seemed transfixed as
she and the bear stood there, with only a screen door between,
evaluating each other.

Then she began to speak. "My, your fur just glistens! You're
beautiful!" My wife was sweet-talking a bear! I couldn't believe it,
and the bear seemed to enjoy it. Sally went on, admiring everything
from the bear's four-inch claws to the large teeth she displayed.
Then turning to us, she called, "Come, come on over and see her!"

We weren't that eager to come closer. After a little bit, the bear
dropped down and exited the porch via the railing. She gathered
her cubs and set off for whatever bear business was on the agenda
that morning.

Suddenly, it dawned on Sally what she had done. Turning to
me, she exclaimed, "I'm free, I'm free!" So she was! Her old fears
were banished.

When we talked later, I asked why she had reacted to the bear
that way. She told me very matter-of-factly, "Why, the Lord
brought the bears. I knew that it was safe." God's grace had deliv-

ered her inwardly. She was indeed free! His continued presence had sustained her through her trial.

The bears continued to visit on occasion, providing us the opportunity to develop a lasting friendship with one of the cubs. But that is a bear story for a future book.

For Sally, this experience altered her attitude about the bears. But let me ask you: Did God draw close to us that day and work a miracle? Or had Sally simply become aware of His continual presence with us? Friends, it is our awareness of God's continual presence with us that opens the avenues of the heart to see and understand the mighty workings of God in our behalf.

## MY CONSTANT COMPANION

You see, most of us hold a concept of God in which God sits on His throne in heaven and inclines an ear to us occasionally, altering the events of life in response to our requests. Most of us view God as somewhat aloof, like earthly monarchs who are willing to come to our aid if needed but who rarely mingle with the commoners. Visit any surviving kingdom and talk to the subjects, and you will find they feel ill at ease in the immediate presence of the royal family.

Even so, if you were able to read the hearts and thoughts of your fellow humans, you would find that many, if not most, people are uncomfortable with the idea of an ever-present God. When we grasp the reality of God as our constant Companion, we experience a corresponding change in behavior and attitude. Behavior that might take place outside the context of a king's presence ceases to occur when he is visible. This is, after all, the normal reaction of a person who has come to an understanding that he is in the presence of one greater than himself. Those who find this environment uncomfortable, who will not uphold a higher standard, will distance themselves from the king.

However much the sinner may wish to avoid God or deny His existence, it is still impossible to hide from God. When Adam and Eve sinned, they, in their panic, tried to hide from the Creator. Yet God did not destroy them. He sought them out and continued to love and care for them.

Alcohol, drugs, immorality, materialism, and intellectual denial may dull our senses, but they will never let us do the impossible. The Bible is filled with stories of individuals who tried to run from God: Adam and Eve, Paul, and Jonah, just to name a few. All failed miserably to hide from God. It's as the Scripture says: "Where can I go from Your Spirit? Or where can I flee from Your presence?" (Ps. 139:7 NKJV).

The Bible says that "God is no respecter of persons" (Acts 10:34 KJV). This means He doesn't treat some people better than others. God does not play favorites. Often people say, "I wish God would speak to me the way He did back in those old Bible times. Things were easier then."

Friends, it is no harder today! If Enoch, Elijah, and Paul could walk with God, then you can too. If God desires to go through each day with Jim Hohnberger, who is one of the slowest learners and one of the most stubborn men on Earth—if God is willing to guide and direct such a man as I with my strong German will and temper—then God desires to be your Companion and Guide too!

If it is so easy, then why do we struggle? Why is it that so few ever find God as a constant Companion? The problem we face is one of attitude. We humans are so used to running our own affairs that we resist the guidance of our loving heavenly Father. We need the attitude of Samuel, who said, "Speak, for Your servant hears" (1 Sam. 3:10 NKJV).

This posture is one of complete dependence on a Guide who sees and knows that which we do not. It is our lack of willingness to listen to God's voice that denies us His guidance. It is our lack of pli-

ability in obeying His voice that causes the Christian life to be so oner-
ous. We are so used to being in control that even when we attempt to
be sensitive to God's Spirit, we tend to discount His leading.

## BAM! SMASH!

The tendency to trust my own knowledge over God's guiding almost
cost me everything beautiful we see about us. Traveling in New
Zealand some years ago, I was a passenger in the front seat of a van.
New Zealand is a beautiful country, and I was enjoying the sight of
the mountains, farms, and sheep. Unexpectedly, I felt the still, small
voice of the Spirit prompting me to close my eyes and rest for a little
while. It was only 10:30 in the morning, and I pushed the thought
away because, as usual, I thought I knew better than God.

Have you ever reacted this way to God's guidance? Fortunately,
God did not leave me alone when I ignored Him, and again the
impression came to rest my eyes for a while. Even though I am a
slow learner, I do eventually catch on, and remembering past experiences, such as the log that almost killed me, I was willing to consider this second prompting.

I shut my eyes and laid my head back, still doubtful that there
was any purpose for this prompting. BAM! SMASH! I felt small
particles of what had been the windshield moments before shower
all over me. A rock had fallen off a nearby hillside and had struck
the window directly in front of me. Unlike American anti-shatter
glass, this window shattered into tiny glass fragments that were all
through my hair, in my ears, down my shirt, even in my nostrils. I
sat there and quivered.

I knew that once more the Lord had spared me serious injury.
He had saved my eyesight! What a good God we serve! I shuddered
at the idea that once again, I had almost ignored His leading. There
with my eyes still shut, I thanked God that I have Him as a constant

Companion in my life. I am so very thankful He is not a mere spectator but is with me in all my trials, all my daily activities.

Jesus wants to pilot you and me through our walk on this earth. We can count on Him, because where we are—God is!

## EVER-PRESENT AND EVER-DEPENDENT— HIS PART AND MINE

When a person becomes convinced that God is ever-present with him, then it is that God can perform great miracles for him. So it was for the three Hebrew captives described in Daniel 3. They had been summoned to appear at the dedication of a great golden image, which King Nebuchadnezzar had set up. All were expected to bow before this image of the king, and everyone did—except Shadrach, Meshach, and Abed-Nego.

The king was enraged at their open defiance and threatened them with a hellish death if they again refused to obey. They would be bound and tossed into a fiery furnace to die in the flames as an example to all of what happens to those who refuse to obey the king.

They calmly replied, "If that is the case, our God whom we serve is able to deliver us from the burning fiery furnace, and He will deliver us from your hand, O king" (Dan. 3:17 NKJV). They expressed no despair at the situation they found themselves in, no faithless timidity; just a quiet, total confidence that God would be with them.

Their response so angered King Nebuchadnezzar that he ordered the furnace made hotter than ever and had the three young men thrown in. It was a brash action prompted by an out-of-control temper used to having its own way, and it cost him several of his strongest soldiers, who died from the heat as they tossed the captives into the furnace.

The king did not have long to enjoy his triumph over these

defiant Hebrews. Upon glancing in the furnace he exclaimed, "Look! . . . I see four men loose, walking in the midst of the fire; and they are not hurt, and the form of the fourth is like the Son of God" (Dan. 3:25 NKJV). When the crisis came, God was there at their side, a visible presence to encourage, guide, and protect. He had been there all along.

Heaven is no farther away today than it was then, but God can do little for us when we lose a sense of our constant dependence on Him. The story of the three Hebrews is a vivid demonstration of what the life of faith is all about. They were ever-dependent upon a power outside of themselves and constantly yielded to the still, small voice of the One who walked with them.

## LORD, NO!

While writing this book, I again experienced the power of an ever-present God and His protecting hand. It had been a wet fall with day after day of heavy rain. The ground was saturated. The night before Sally and I were to fly to Dallas, Texas, the rain changed to snow, and, by early morning, an inch of snow was on the ground. Unfortunately, with so much water on the gravel road, it froze into a slippery mass of ice and stone.

Living in the wilderness makes it necessary to leave our house in the predawn hours in order to make our morning flights. This particular trip found us on the road at four-thirty in the morning. Driving down the familiar wilderness road that led toward civilization, we came to a sharp, horseshoe-shaped, descending curve and started to slide.

When you start to slide in a four-wheel drive vehicle with antilock brakes, you don't slide to one side or the other, but rather the vehicle slides straight forward without any vestige of control.

At this point in the road, "straight forward" meant a rather intimate acquaintance with some large cottonwood trees. If we managed to miss those trees, we would fare no better, for the hillside at that point was so steeply angled that we would no doubt travel only a short distance before our Ford Explorer would roll 360 degrees all the way to the creek below.

I could picture in my mind's eye the jarring impact with those trees and the instantaneous airbag deployment. I called out, "Lord, no!" and then we left the road at forty miles per hour.

Suddenly, we stopped. The Explorer rested well off the road on a steep hillside. Those cottonwood trees were only inches from Sally's door. Stepping gingerly out of the vehicle, I took a flashlight and examined our position. The truck was so sharply angled that one wheel was actually off the ground.

Walking back up to the road, I examined our tire tracks and could not humanly explain our good fortune. The tire tracks headed directly toward the trees, yet something or someone had pushed us aside at the last possible moment. There was no natural obstacle—the slope should have pushed us even more solidly into the trees—but an ever-present God had saved us. Hours later, when the wrecker from town managed to save our truck by winching it sideways away from the trees, we found there wasn't even a scratch on the vehicle.

All of us, myself included, need to pray for and cultivate an increasing awareness, a more perfect consciousness of God's presence with us. Then we will be more likely to respond to His overtures and guidance. When we are aware of His presence, our hearts will commune more readily with Him and come to know Him in ever-increasing degrees. Our cooperation will become more perfect through faith, love, and practice. Yet it will require a lot of courage to wrench us loose from the grip of our times.

One of the most endearing terms for Jesus in all of Scripture is *Immanuel,* which means "God with us." We need to learn that God is not in some far-removed heavenly place, occasionally looking down on us. No, when Jesus left the earth, He promised to send the Comforter, God's Spirit, that He might be always with us (John 16:7).

Now that is a comfort to me. Today, I no longer pray to a God in some distant place, but I recognize Him as my constant Companion. And He is!

# Chapter Six

# SEEING HIM WHO
# IS INVISIBLE

For he endured as seeing Him who is invisible.
*Hebrews 11:27 NKJV*

AFTER THE BATTLE of Gettysburg, General Robert E. Lee happened upon an officer who was analyzing some of the mistakes of the three-day conflict.

"Young man," responded Lee, "why did you not tell me that before the battle? Even as stupid a man as I am can see it all now."

Most of us accept Lee's premise that 20/20 hindsight is an inevitable part of life, but still there are those memories—uncomfortable memories of what might have been . . . if only. If only we could have known then what we know now. Who among us can look back at our life history without a twinge of pain at the mistakes made or feelings of regret over the foolish errors in judgment, the missed blessings, the lost opportunities?

Even as you read these lines, the moments pass, one by one, into eternity, etching as they go a record that you will look back on in the future. Will your future history be as full of regrets as your past has been?

Friends, I wish there were a way I could show you a movie of my life as a Christian. No one ever taught me these things that I am sharing with you. It took me years—literally years—of trial and error to figure out each one of these principles for myself.

By now, you understand I was not satisfied with a simply intellectual knowledge, but rather I desired truth that had a practical application to my life. I hope I can fire that same desire within your soul. That excites me, for religion apart from practical, daily—in fact, moment by moment—application to the life is nearly useless.

In the early days of the Christian church, our religion was strong and vital. It changed lives so completely that people stood in awe. It was a religion with power. It is here that the churches of our day have failed their membership and violated the very reason for their existence. Why is it that all the Christian churches have so many new converts turn from them in disgust? Why is it that so few of the youth in the churches seem to hold on to the faith? Why is it that religion makes only minimal differences in the divorce rates among Christian couples as compared to the rates among non-Christian couples? Have you ever stopped to honestly ask yourself these questions?

Church leaders have, and their answers have spawned a slew of programs in the church designed to address these areas of weakness. And so many of them are dismal failures! Why? Because they attempt to deal with the symptoms rather than the problem. The great plague in Christianity is that few—very, very few—of those who claim to be Christians—very, very few, even among those who are ministers—possess a gospel capable of transforming their whole lives.

That was a bold statement. So let me demonstrate.

Once I was invited to speak to a group of ministers. I am just a lay preacher, not a professional minister. What should I say when addressing the "experts"? As I stood at that podium, I said, "I wish that every time a minister stood in the pulpit, a big screen would come down behind him and show how he led his life in the preceding week—how he acted in his home with his children and his wife, how he responded to temptations and trials. Would you get up and preach if those were the conditions?"

"No!" the ministers responded.

"Then my friends, you have not found the gospel. Jesus would have had no problem with such a condition, nor should we. He knew His actions were just as straight and pure as His doctrines.

"I am not saying we should all be spiritual supermen who never fail, but God's desire for us is that failure should be the exception rather than the rule in our lives. Further, when we do fail, He wants us to get back up and continue on our lives' journeys with Him, not wallow in self-pity.

"I have always shared true stories of my life, including my own failures, in speaking to others of Christianity. They have become the favorite part of the seminars I participate in, and the reason is that people are attracted to and relate to people who share their weaknesses. More importantly, many are hungry, just as I was, for someone to share what Christianity looks like in the real world, not just at church.

"The problem comes when failure is the rule in our homes rather than the exception. When it is the exception, we don't mind the camera, and when it isn't, we don't want anyone to see. The challenge for you men of God is to make the gospel a living, breathing reality in your own homes, and then you can bring it into your churches."

The history of the early church is recorded in the Acts of the Apostles. Actions—not Doctrines of the Apostles, not Beliefs of the Apostles, not Sermons of the Apostles, but Actions—these are the mark of the true gospel: "Ye shall know them by their fruits" (Matt. 7:16 KJV).

Dear reader, would you be willing to be put under such scrutiny? If not, then I challenge you to do something different with this book from what you have done with any other book you have read. What you hold in your hands is a workbook for a project that you are going to build in your own life. It is up to you, the reader, to take the experiences described here and make them part of your experience. Take the thoughts presented and mull them over, chew on them, assimilate them in a practical way, until they become your own.

It requires very little for you to live a life like this. You need only to cultivate a sense of God's presence with you throughout the day, and then you must be motivated to act on His guidance. Too simple? Watch and see.

## A LACK OF FULL DISCLOSURE

I got a phone call one evening from a man I had met several years before. He and his family had visited us to see our wilderness property and our lifestyle. We shared with them about the practical gospel we were applying to our lives, but they just weren't that interested. Now he was on the phone, saying, "Jim, I'd like your family to come to our place for a weekend. I know you have come to understand the practical gospel, and we need a little help with the family and the marriage."

I told him I would pray about it. Afterward, feeling that I had the Lord's permission to do so, I called Rob back, and we set up a date to visit them.

Arriving on a Friday evening, Rob wanted me to go for a walk with him. You see, Rob hadn't told me the whole story. He hadn't given what a lawyer might call "full disclosure." It turned out that just prior to his call to me, Rob's wife had told him that she was finished with him. She wasn't mad at him. It was just over. There were no feelings left. She planned to leave him and take the children.

Rob had asked her if she would stay if he really changed. She consented that if he would really change, then she would consider it. So Rob had a weekend in which to transform himself if he wanted to save his marriage.

"Rob," I said once the whole story had come out, "the God I have come to know in the mountains—His gospel is so powerful I guarantee that you can be a new creature in Christ by Sunday. But Rob," I continued, "I cannot guarantee that your wife won't leave you."

"Well, what do I do?" he asked.

"Simply take this one text and apply it to your life. It is found in James 1:19: 'Let every man be swift to hear, slow to speak, slow to wrath'" (NKJV).

Rob looked at me like, *So?* It was almost as if he said, "I've read that lots of times, and *that* is supposed to save my marriage?"

Well, that's just the problem many of us have with the Scriptures. We read them and go on our way, never stopping to think about what they mean in a practical application to our lives.

I went on, "Rob, what does it mean to 'let every man be swift to hear'? It means that you are going to have to cultivate a sensitivity to hear the voice of God, an awareness of God's presence with you throughout the day. For the first time in your life, you're going to have to let someone else guide your actions. You are going to have to learn to take each situation and filter what you know and see through the unseen God who knows that which you do not.

"Everything in this world is designed to intrude upon faith in an invisible God. The visible world is the enemy of the invisible God. The visible world clamors for your attention, intrudes upon your senses, and insists that you listen to it. You will have to break this habit and instead listen to the voice of God: 'Your ears shall hear a word behind you, saying, "This is the way, walk in it"' (Isa. 30:21 NKJV).

"Now, Rob, what about that 'slow to speak?' It means that we filter our every word through God, that He may guide us."

Rob had not been in the habit of filtering his words. In fact, that was one of the main reasons he was in such trouble with his wife. I could relate—I had been there—but now I could speak from the perspective of having seen the difference this filtering process made.

I remember one morning I had been working in the garage, cleaning and sharpening one of my chain saws. After filling it with gas and oil, I returned it to its proper place, ready for use in the future. I enjoy working with my hands, but I dislike the smell of petroleum products on my skin, so before I started a new project, I walked to the back door of the cabin that is close to a bathroom where I could wash my hands.

Lathering my hands, I was happy and having a good day with the Lord. "Whatcha doing, dear?" a sweet voice queried from the doorway.

I glanced up to see Sally looking in on me. Immediately, I could feel my flesh want to rise up and say, "What do you mean? Can't you see I'm washing my hands? That's a stupid question!" In the past I would have said all that and more. My marriage would have suffered. But while my flesh was rising, I could hear the quiet voice of God saying, "Treat her gently, Jim." Which voice am I going to listen to: the voice of the flesh that wants to complain about her silly question, or the voice of God? I am so thankful I chose to say, "Washing my hands, dear."

"That's fine, honey. I was just wondering how your day was going," my sweet wife responded, the harmony between us unbroken.

Men, why is it that after we marry our wives, we want them to do everything and phrase everything exactly as we would? We need to understand that in our wives, the Lord has brought a beautiful difference and balance into our lives. I wouldn't have phrased the inquiry the same way she did, but the very reason I was attracted to my wife was that she thinks, acts, looks, and even smells different from Jim Hohnberger. That, gentlemen, is good news!

So, I want all you men to know that my marriage—more importantly, my attitude toward the wonderful person I am married to—improved drastically once I recognized and learned to treasure these differences. If you want to improve your marriage, learn to cultivate a sense of God's presence with you, and respond to it. It works every time, but Rob had yet to discover this.

"Now, Rob, let's look at the last part of the text," I continued. "'Slow to wrath' means that even when our wives and children provoke us, we choose to remain in Christ and let His Spirit, rather than the passions of the moment, control us. We choose to surrender these upset feelings to God and allow Him to remove them from our lives before they damage the ones we love."

Rob and I had been on a long walk by this time—a walk punctuated by more than a few tears. He went to bed that night with a lot to think about! And so began one of the most extraordinary weekends I have ever experienced.

When we awoke the next day, I wondered how it would go. I prayed for this couple no human could help, but with whom the Almighty was striving. There was a beautiful breakfast spread before us that morning, and as we sat at the table, I noticed a large dish of steaming oatmeal in front of Rob. As soon as the blessing was said, Rob stood and began to serve himself the oatmeal. The self-serving, me-first attitude just seemed to flow from him.

I sat there wondering if Rob had considered filtering his actions through God when suddenly, he stopped what he was doing, paused for just a moment, and then handed the bowl to my son. He then served my other son, my wife, me, and then his wife and his children. As he did this, I ventured a glance at his wife. She was staring, open-mouthed, at her husband.

You know, I truly believe that in their entire marriage, this was the only time she had ever seen Rob serve anyone but himself first. Rob was becoming swift to hear. The Spirit of the Lord was manifesting Himself to Rob's consciousness, and Rob was beginning to cooperate with Him who is invisible.

A little later on in the meal, his five-year-old daughter, who was used to running the household, rudely—and I mean rudely—interrupted her father while he was speaking. Remember what Rob and I had talked about the night before, being slow to speak and slow to wrath? Well, this certainly wasn't Rob's natural inclination, and he demonstrated it by responding to his daughter in harshness and anger.

Then he abruptly fell silent. I have never seen someone do what he did next, but he just bowed his head right there in front of us all for a moment, and when he looked up at his daughter, it was in the Spirit of God. Everyone there could see the difference. His daughter was astonished when he said, "I'm sorry," and began to reason with her about her behavior. Once more, I looked at his wife and found her astonished at the changes in her "hopeless" husband. I was sitting there watching this, and even I could hardly believe the contrast.

I was seeing this man's life being transformed before my very eyes! The invisible God was guiding and instructing this failure of a husband, and by allowing that process, Rob was working out his salvation "with fear and trembling; for it is God who works in you both to will and to do for *His* good pleasure" (Phil. 2:12–13 NKJV).

I wish I could take time to share the whole weekend with you because it continued like that. It was marvelous! Finally, during a discussion near the end of the weekend, Rob had an opportunity to deliver one of those zingers to his wife. You know, just a cute little sarcasm at which everybody laughs, but at which the wife aches and cries inside because she's been jabbed.

When this goes on year after year, finally, she becomes so hardened that there are just no feelings left, and she wants a divorce. In the silence that followed his inconsiderate jab, Rob looked at his wife and in a moment of honesty exclaimed, "Why do I do this to you? I have been doing this to you all the years of our married life. Will you for-give me?" You could just see the remorse and self-loathing on his face. There were tears in her eyes, for, finally, she was a prisoner of hope.

Sunday afternoon, just we four adults gathered alone. I wanted to know what she would do. Would she leave him? No, she had decided she wouldn't. "Finally I see a little glimmer of hope that maybe this thing can work out," she responded. We left them with hope for the future, but also the knowledge of how easily Satan can derail a new experience.

Hope is all many of us want, just a hint of hope that things can work out, whether our problem is a marriage gone bad, or being a single parent, or something totally different.

Moses had problems too. He was charged with leading a whole nation of Jim Hohnbergers to the promised land. A whole nation of stubborn, self-willed individuals. I wouldn't wish that job on any-body! But Moses "endured as seeing Him who is invisible" (Heb. 11:27 NKJV). He learned to view the visible—the lack of food, the absence of water, the rebellions, the snakes, the idolatry—through the eyes of the invisible God. When he did this, all problems sank in obscurity. Nothing was too hard for God!

If we would cultivate this skill and trust in Him who knows and sees all, we would see more of God's hand in the providences of our lives.

## WON'T TAKE NO FOR AN ANSWER

After more than two years in the wilderness, I knew I would have to eventually find some type of employment, but as of yet it was not clear what I should do. I believed that my all-knowing heavenly Father knew what course I should take. Still, this was early on in my experience, and I had a hard time following His leading. God had to be persistent to get my attention.

While doing some errands in town, I happened to run into the owner of the local real estate office. We had worked with Paul when we first contemplated moving to Montana. Even though he had been unable to help us, he was a typically friendly westerner and greeted me warmly. Then he said, "You know, I've been thinking about you lately. I'm considering expanding my office's dealing in rural and wilderness property, and I think you should come work for me."

I thanked him but turned the idea down. After all, I had spent most of my life in sales, and I knew that selling real estate would require me to spend time in the office and attend sales meetings. I would have to get a license, and I couldn't sell property without a phone. At that time, the only phone service in our valley was radiotelephone, and this was so cost prohibitive that there was no sense in even considering it.

But the idea wouldn't go away, and soon it seemed that every time I went to town, I saw Paul in a store or on the street, and always he encouraged me to consider working for him. Finally, I agreed to meet with him and discuss the possibilities. I was still sure that it was a waste of time, but it was becoming clear that Paul would not be denied until I was able to demonstrate to him just how impractical this idea was. Soon I found myself seated with Sally across from Paul in his office.

"So, what is it going to take to get you to come work for me, Jim?"

"Well," I began, "I am not licensed. You would have to pay all my expenses to become licensed, including my books and examination fees."

Paul just nodded, so I continued. "When I came up to the mountains, I worked very hard to get control of my time. If I am going to come on board, you must promise me that I will never be required to attend any meetings. I must be allowed to work just as much or as little as I desire. You would also have to pay any association fees and cover all my advertising costs."

"Is that all you want, Jim?"

"No. You will have to set up and pay for all the expenses related to a radiotelephone line at my house."

"Is that it?" he asked.

"Yes," I responded.

"Great!" With scarcely concealed triumph, he reached into his desk drawer, pulled out two books, and handed them over to me. I found myself holding the study guides for the licensing exam.

"You're crazy!" I finally managed to blurt out. I had offered him the worst deal in the world. No businessman would lay out that kind of money with no guarantee of a return.

Paul just smiled at me and said, "Let me know when you're ready to take the exam." Only later did I learn that Paul had checked me out with some business associates in Wisconsin. They told him, "Jim Hohnberger does his best work by himself. You just leave him alone, and he'll do fine."

Belatedly realizing that God had been altering events and trying to get my attention, I decided the only avenue open to me was to approach real estate sales in the same manner I was trying to approach my whole life, which was: "Lord, what would Thou have me to do?" So when I met with a client, I appealed to the Lord to guide me in my choice of property to show him or her, and the Lord blessed my dependence upon Him.

I told Paul he was crazy, but was he? Soon I was the number-one grossing agent in the office, and our office became first in the state. To think I had nearly discarded the idea of selling real estate.

Independence from God has always been the curse of Jim Hohnberger's life. I am learning day by day to become less and less trustful of self, and I pray that the Lord will make me more sensitive to His Spirit's leading. Unfortunately, I am such a slow learner that I sometimes despair that I will ever get it. You see, God desires to guide each of us on the pathway of life, but sometimes His guidance doesn't seem to make sense to us, except in hindsight.

## WILL I EVER LEARN?

"Jim, will you go up to the greenhouse and close it for the night before you go on your walk?" Sally asked me one evening.

"Sure," I said, heading out the door and up the hill to the greenhouse. The greenhouse must be ventilated on warm days to keep it from overheating. Still, nights in the mountains can be chilly even in summer, so the vents must be closed to protect the tender plants. It was six in the evening when I finished shutting things up for the night.

I usually take a short walk by the river in the evening. This helps me unwind and relax before our family time at six-thirty. That night, I changed my mind and decided to walk along the back edge of our property rather than going down by the river.

Setting out, I felt an impression upon my mind: "Jim, you need to tell your wife where you are going. You might be mauled by a grizzly bear." This seemed a little silly, so I reasoned it away. Again, the same impression came, and again I pushed it aside, but I was uneasy and still wrestling with it in my mind.

Perhaps a word of explanation is in order. My property is truly wilderness, and you don't have to be very far from my home to be lost from sight. I usually walked by the river, so in walking back in the woods, I was departing from my usual pattern. If I turned up missing, my family would naturally look by the river, not in the woods. Whether telling Sally or not would have had any effect upon what follows is impossible to say because I didn't, but the knowledge that I hadn't certainly added to my stress at the time.

After walking about two hundred yards, I came to a sharp little drop in elevation on my property known as a bench. Just as I started down this incline, I felt a chill that had nothing to do with the weather. Looking about, I saw a female grizzly bear with cubs. She was standing up on her haunches thirty or forty feet to my left and staring right at me.

Now when a bear stares at you, it doesn't just stand there and stare. Because bears don't see well, they shift a little, back and forth, trying to focus and sort of look right through you. It is about the most disconcerting and frightening experience you can imagine.

Looking at that bear, the story of Elisha and the disrespectful boys whom God punished with two she-bears raced through my mind. Those two bears spanked, so to speak, forty-two boys. (2 Kings 2:23-24) I couldn't help but wonder if I was about to be spanked for failing to listen to that still, small voice of God's Spirit.

I looked around at the trees nearby and thought, *There is no way I can make it!* Besides, I intuitively knew that I had to approach this visible problem through the power of the invisible.

Jesus said, "My sheep hear My voice, and I know them, and they follow Me" (John 10:27 NKJV). I realized that it was not enough to know that God was speaking to me. It was not enough to recognize His desire to lead in my life. I had to follow Him, and here it was that I had failed. I prayed, "Lord, forgive me! What would You have me to do now?"

"Duck down, Jim, below the level of the bench so she can't see you. Then go *fast* to the guest cabin." This was the impression I had, so I dropped down to the bottom of the bench and began to move quickly toward the guest cabin. But even at this point, I didn't fully obey. Thank God He doesn't abandon us just because we fail to listen. What a long-suffering God we serve!

My mother has always told me, "Jim, that curiosity of yours is going to get you in big trouble someday." Well, as I was running along the bottom of that little hill, I wondered what the bear was doing. After all, nothing was biting at my rear end as I ran. In obeying the impression to go to the guesthouse, I had turned my back on the bear, and I hate having my back to a grizzly.

I was about halfway to the guesthouse when I spotted a stump up on top of the bench, and I decided that I would climb up there to check out what the bear was doing. Looking back, I found she wasn't where I expected her to be. The place she had been was empty except for her cubs, which she had sent up a tree. They were squalling away in that Douglas fir tree, but they stayed out of Mom's way while she dealt with me.

Glancing about, I saw her standing up on her haunches in the place I had just left, and she was looking right at me. I knew bears well enough by that time to know she was going to charge me. She heard her cubs crying in that tree, and the fire in her eyes told me she was not pleased with Jim Hohnberger! I looked at the guesthouse, and I told myself, *There is no way I can make it!*

Do you have any idea how fast grizzly bears can run? They run a lot faster than I can, even with a lot of adrenaline in my system! Psalm 34:6 says, "This poor man cried out, and the LORD heard him, and saved him out of all his troubles" (NKJV). Now that's the kind of God I want to serve! Don't you? A God who saves those who cry unto Him.

In distress and self-disgust, I prayed, "Lord, will I *ever* learn?"

"Just hold still, Jim. You'll be OK."

As I watched, the bear dropped down to all fours and grunted for her cubs. At least they knew how to obey and came running. It was only June, and they were still very young, little more than two balls of fluff, but by the end of the summer, they would be well on their way to becoming just as fearsome predators as their mother. With her cubs by her side once more, the bear turned to me and snorted her disgust before ambling off into the woods.

We can learn to break the habit of ignoring the invisible presence of the Lord only through the medium of faith. Each of us needs to develop a spiritual awareness until it becomes the most important thing in our lives, the thing to which we cling for direction.

I'm not the only one who heads for trouble when I lose the perspective of an ever-present God. My family suffers too. It has always been this way from the moment sin entered the world. When Eve came to Adam with the forbidden fruit, he knew she had disobeyed God. Yet Adam thought that he loved Eve so much that the very idea of separation was impossible to contemplate. He chose to eat of the fruit in order to remain with her, even if their only future together was death.

Watch how his attitude changed once his will and ways were not surrendered to God. When confronted with his own actions, Adam blamed Eve, then blamed God for creating her! "The woman whom You gave to be with me, she gave me of the tree, and I ate" (Gen. 3:12 NKJV).

I have found that it is usually my spouse who bears the brunt of my frustration when I lose sight of the presence of God with me. However, I have also found that nothing has so improved my marriage as learning to filter the *seen*, my words and actions, through the influence of the *unseen*, God.

## JUST SMILE, JIM

Things have changed a lot in the years since I started selling wilderness real estate. I work exclusively for God now, speaking and writing, sharing those things He has taught me. Our family gets invited to speak about the gospel in many different locations all over the globe.

We had just flown home after sixty days in Australia and New Zealand. We met many wonderful people in those countries and ministered to their needs. We often stay with the families that invite us, and we had not eaten a meal by ourselves—just the four of us—

in those sixty days. We flew into Kalispel, Montana, exhausted. We felt like towels that had been put through an old-fashioned wringer washing machine. All the energy had been wrung out, and we longed for solitude and the simple pleasure of a meal in privacy.

Heading up the North Fork Road, we found over two feet of snow on the ground. With the truck in four-wheel drive, we drove home and into our driveway. By this time the snow was so deep, the truck was pushing it out in front of us. Pulling up to the house, I asked Sally to go in and start the woodstove and prepare a simple meal.

"Matthew," I said, "I will unload the car if you will take the things I bring in and put them away." He agreed, and lastly I asked Andrew to go to the garage and get the snowblower out and clear the snow from the walkways and the area around the garage. Everyone went about his or her job, and soon the pleasant smell of food greeted me whenever I stepped into the house with belongings from the car.

It's true: many hands make light work. The car was empty, and I stepped outside to check under the seats to make sure I didn't forget anything. I could see Andrew over by the garage finishing up with the snowblower and getting ready to put it away. I trained my boys that tools should not be put away dirty but rather should be put away so that they are ready for use. This means that we refuel things like the chain saws and fill them with oil. It means that we take a broom and sweep all the snow out of the snowblower before we put it back in the garage.

True to his training, Andrew got the very expensive Fuller Brush broom to clean the snowblower. The machine was still running, and it seemed to him that he could just jam the broom in quickly and jerk it back out to knock the snow loose. This would save him the effort of shutting down the engine and starting it all over again just to drive it into the garage. Like the rest of us, he was exhausted from our sixty days' effort.

I was busy feeling under the seat when I heard the terrible clatter of metal against metal. I didn't have to even raise my head to know what had happened. When I did look, I saw that the tines had grabbed the broom and twisted it until the metal handle looked like a corkscrew. Andrew was down on his knees, trying to extract the broom. I found myself walking quickly toward my son with words of rebuke on the tip of my tongue. When I stood by him, he wouldn't look up at me. He was perhaps fearful of my reaction.

Think about it for a minute. We had just returned from preaching the practical gospel on the other side of the world, and he was concerned, and rightly so, about his father's reaction. I am so thankful that he didn't look up right away. It gave me a few blessed moments to hear the voice of God say, "Jim, have you asked Me what I'd have you to do?"

"Well, no, Lord. I know what he did wrong, and I thought I would give him a little lecture, so he will learn from this mistake," I said, excusing myself.

"Just smile at him, Jim."

"Just smile? You have got to be kidding, Lord! Why, that was my expensive broom he just ruined!"

"Just smile, Jim. The natural consequences were sufficient." Of course, this all happened in a fraction of a second. It takes longer to read about it than it did to occur. Andrew looked up at that point, and I smiled at him and said, "Come on. Let's go eat."

Later at the table, as we were eating, Andrew said, "Father?"

"Yes, son."

"I'm sorry. It was a stupid thing to do."

You know, we have all done foolish things in our lives. The Lord was right. The natural consequences of his action were sufficient to prevent any reoccurrence. Andrew would never do something like that again. If I had lectured as my flesh wanted to, the lesson might well have been lost. His focus could easily have become defending himself against Father's wrath rather than learning self-government. What would Andrew have thought of the gospel I believe and had preached for sixty days if that message had been unable to keep me from uttering words I would have regretted? I know what he would have concluded, and he would have been right!

That is the problem in Christianity today. Many youth see that their parents' religion, behind closed doors, is vain, and when they are old enough, they walk away from such useless religion. In such cases, it shouldn't surprise us because we haven't learned to recognize God's invisible presence with us and to yield to His gentle entreaties.

God desires us to apply these principles in all our interpersonal relationships, be it with friends or strangers that we meet on the street, but does that include those who do not treat us kindly? I leave you to judge.

## MY RIGHTS AND WRONGS

When one lives up in the mountains, a four-wheel drive is not a luxury, not a fashionable vehicle of suburban mothers, but an absolute necessity if one must be mobile in the winter. I have to depend on the vehicle not to strand my wife or family in the wilderness, so I am sensitive to the mechanical needs of my vehicle.

When it was time to replace my Toyota Land Cruiser, I went into town and purchased a new sport utility vehicle. Shortly after I purchased it, I started hearing a sound from one of my front hubs. It was not a good sound to hear coming from a four-wheel-drive, so I took it to the dealer, and he gladly replaced the hub as the truck was still under warranty.

Toward the end of the warranty, I noticed the same type of sound starting to come from the other front hub. Knowing what was wrong this time, I made an appointment to have it examined at the dealership where I purchased the truck.

You must understand that it is a weakness in my character to become irritated when things go wrong. Realizing this, I go to great lengths to make sure that things run smoothly. This way I help to decrease temptations to lose self-control and become irritated. With this in mind, I made my appointment at the dealership so that it was the very first one of the day, at 8:00 AM. I explained the problem to the assistant service manager and asked him how long he felt it would take.

"About an hour," he responded.

I decided to take a walk around town and do a few errands. I planned my morning so I would not arrive back at the dealership until 9:15 AM. That way I was sure the car would be done, and I would have no opportunity to become frustrated because it wasn't ready.

When I returned to pick up my car, I noticed it was still in the same place I had left it. It was possible that it had been parked there after servicing, but it made me a little uneasy, and with a sense of foreboding I entered the service department. "Is it all set?" I asked the assistant service manager as I came up to the counter.

"Haven't had a chance to bring it in," he responded.

I could feel the frustration building in my flesh. "When do you think you will be able to look at it?"

"I'm not sure. I really don't think it's a problem, Jim."

Again, I could feel my frustration level rise. I wanted to straighten him out and defend my rights. I am thankful the Lord is an ever-present help in time of danger—I was in danger, not from the service manager, but from my own flesh, which wanted to have control of me right then.

"Surrender it to Me," the Lord whispered in my thoughts.

"All right, Lord, You can have this frustration."

In a reasonable voice I asked, "How would you know there is nothing wrong if you haven't even looked at it? Would you at least consent to take it out and drive it? The noise is unmistakable."

He grudgingly agreed to drive it and was back in a very short time. "I don't think it's anything," he said matter-of-factly.

"Didn't you hear the noise?" I asked.

"Yeah, I heard it. I think it is just the fact that it is in four-wheel drive on the dry pavement, where there would be a little slipping, rather than on the snow."

This was the strangest explanation I had ever heard. "But it is the same sound the other side made when it was bad," I pleaded.

"No, it's different."

"Lord, this isn't fair!" I said silently. "He has prejudged the situation and isn't even being reasonable."

"Just stay in Me, Jim. You don't have to let go of Me, regardless of how others may act toward you."

"If you changed the hub, and the noise went away, wouldn't you agree that that was the problem?" I asked.

"No," he responded.

"No, you wouldn't change the hub, or no, you wouldn't agree that that was the problem?"

"I wouldn't agree to either," he said, becoming annoyed.

"Well, I can't make you change the hub."

"No, you can't," he agreed forcibly.

"I am scheduled to leave for Europe next week, and my wife is going to be here alone with this truck. I'm sure it is the same thing as the other hub. Besides, by the time I return the truck will be off warranty."

"That's your problem!" he responded.

"We just don't agree, do we?" I asked.

"No, we don't."

"I guess all I can do is take it home and bring it back in if it gets worse."

"I guess so," he said. "You can pay over there," he commented, handing me a bill.

I walked toward the cashier's desk with a sinking feeling in my heart. "Lord," I prayed silently, "I have never been treated so unfairly in all my life, and now I am supposed to pay for it too. This is just too much!"

"Trust in Me, Jim, and surrender it all to Me."

Oh, it is so hard when we feel our rights have been trampled, and our flesh wants to straighten out the wrongs that have been done to us.

I didn't know it, but Sam, the service manager, had been watching all of this transpire, and at that point, he approached me. "Jim, are you uncomfortable with the decision that was rendered?"

"Am I ever!" I told him, explaining the whole situation.

"If I bring it in and change the hub, and the noise doesn't go away, are you willing to pay for the labor of putting it on and taking it back off?"

"Certainly," I replied. "But if the sound does go away, are you willing to agree that the hub was the problem and cover it under the warranty?"

Sam agreed, and the truck was brought in. The hub was replaced, and the sound vanished! God had the situation in hand and had a solution there for me all the time. I didn't need to defend myself when the God of the universe was at my side. I simply needed to surrender to Him.

## Oneness with God

Do you, right now, sense the invisible presence of God calling to your heart? He wants to be your present Helper. "Everyone who is of the truth hears My voice" (John 18:37 NKJV). He wants to empower you to live above the pull of the flesh, above the pull of the world. It is when the world sees us being saved in the present rather than just saved from the past that our lives will demonstrate that we have the power of God rather than just a form of godliness.

Today's churches, for the most part, have lost this power, and this is the reason many turn from them. People long for a power able to save them from themselves, a power that makes life here a joy. They desire more than just lame promises of joy in the hereafter.

This experience is within the reach of all. It wasn't until I purposed in my heart daily, hourly, moment by moment to cooperate with the invisible God that my experience blossomed. Today, it continues to flower and produce fruit as I address the visible through the invisible God. I am not writing as one who has arrived, nor as one who has experienced to the fullest the opportunity that awaits him, but as one who is pressing on. "We do not look at the things which are seen, but at the things which are not seen. For the things which are seen are temporary, but the things which are not seen are eternal" (2 Cor. 4:18 NKJV).

When I first began to see and understand this experience, I prayed daily, "Lord, help me to be so sensitive to Your presence that the lightest whisper of Jesus will move my soul." Now I can write as one who is beginning to experience the deeper life and maturing in it. And I'm not the only one. As I travel the globe, I meet others, here and there, who are tasting of the same experience—and you can too.

Many desire this experience, but because it involves continual self-denial, few seem willing to endure the painful death of their own wishes and desires in order to obtain it. It breaks my heart because they come so close, they examine the experience, they feel the pull of the heart for oneness with God. They see that God has been in pursuit of them their whole lives, and they understand the lifestyle changes they should implement to make surrender to God easier. They realize that all their choices must be submitted to Him, and they recognize that God is always with them to lead and direct, if they are willing to follow. But they never change. It has been an intellectual exercise rather than an affair of the heart.

Don't let this happen to you. Rob had been motivated to make this experience real because he was in danger of losing his whole family, but many more are in the same type of danger and do not realize it. What is it going to take to motivate you?

## So What Happened?

Two weeks after our visit with Rob's family, I began to wonder how things were going for them. Had Rob fallen back into his old ways, or was he keeping an awareness of God's presence and submitting to His guidance?

Then Rob called. "Jim, my wife has become my best friend! You will never believe it, but my wife and I have stayed up for the last two weeks talking until late at night. You know, she has something to say. I never knew it. I never gave her the chance. I want to thank you," he said.

"I also want you to know that you are free to use our story to help others see and believe. I didn't know my wife was thinking about leaving. If I didn't know it, then there are other men out there whose wives are thinking about it too."

Rob spoke of the risk of temporal loss, but far worse would be the loss of your spouse or your children to the heavenly kingdom. Do you really believe that they can rise to a higher level of spiritual existence than you yourself practice? Are they worth the effort? Christ thought we were worth that effort, for He said, "For their sakes I sanctify Myself" (John 17:19 NKJV). Shouldn't we do the same for those we love?

Rob was slowly learning in every situation of life to see Him who is invisible and be guided by Him. You and I can possess this experience, too, but we are so used to following inclination and impulse—so used to reacting to the visible world about us—that it will take some retraining to hear the voice of God and to sense His presence in every situation.

Above the chaos of the world, beyond the clamor of emotions, greater than our intellectual knowledge, is the quiet presence of God awaiting only our recognition and cooperation that He may guide, comfort, and direct us. This is the key to a life without regrets.

*Chapter Seven*

# SELECTIVE HEARING

Speak, LORD, for Your servant hears.
*1 Samuel 3:9 NKJV*

SOMETIMES A SIMPLE story from a friend can illustrate divine truth better than any sermon. At least that's how I felt when I heard my friend's story of a unique trail he and his wife had hiked while blindfolded, but let me share it in his words.

> My hands slid along the rope as my feet took slow, tentative steps. They were so slow that my five-year-old guide could easily outpace me. With each step came an awareness that I had entered a world where darkness reigned and hearing was the most precious of senses.
>
> The forty-degree weather chilled my hands, but I resisted the urge to pull on my gloves for fear of losing even more sensory input. My hands, more than my feet, told of passing distance as the guide rope slid gently through them. An occasional knot announced the completion of another rope length. I could sense turns only from the angle changes in the rope.
>
> The scents of raw earth so recently exposed by the melting

snows accompanied me as I walked, and the sweet smell of cedar trees announced their presence along the trail. Most of the odors were warm and friendly—then I caught the scent of carrion. *It's probably a dead deer,* I thought. The odor was strong, and I realized the carcass was very near. It made me nervous that perhaps we might startle a bear awakened by the warm spell and drawn to the smell of death.

As I walked, I became increasingly dependent upon my ears. The crunch of snow underfoot warned me of slippery conditions. The gurgling sound of a mountain brook growing closer by the moment set me to wondering if I would accidentally step into the icy water.

But by far the most reassuring sound was the voice of my son who, at five years of age, was acting as my guide. "There is more snow here, Daddy," or "Watch out for this stump!" he warned. I smiled inwardly, thinking, *I can't "watch out" for anything.* Then suddenly, I ran into him. He had intentionally placed himself in front of the stump to protect me from danger. My utter dependence upon him was awkward and scary.

Sometimes we walked in silence, and, after a little while, I feared that he had moved on ahead and left me to struggle alone with the unseen obstacles. I called out only to find he was right beside me. "Please don't leave me," I said pleadingly. Without his eyes, I could only grope my way along the guideline. With his vision, I could walk confident that he would warn and protect me from danger. "Oh, Daddy, I would never leave you!" he exclaimed, incredulous that I could even contemplate such a thought.

At length, I came to the end of the rope, the end of my journey. I removed my blindfold only to be dazzled by the light of day. After I adjusted and could focus once more, I saw the smiling face of my guide beaming up at me, serene in the confidence that he could see me through.

I may not have walked the course my friend did, but I've lived this experience of stumbling along through life, groping for direction, and yet God wants to guide you and me in exactly the same way. We may have little confidence in Him. We probably have never trusted Him completely our whole lives. Maybe we haven't even known personally anyone who trusted God that way. Yet He is not discouraged. He knows that by our very nature, we are inclined to refuse His guidance. And still God stands ready to assist, confident just like that little boy that He can do the job.

You see, God knows all the problems, all the heartaches that we will face in this life, and He has a solution for every one of them. Better, far better than just a solution to our problems is the fact that the God of the universe is in sympathy with our struggles. The Bible says, "For we do not have a High Priest who cannot sympathize with our weaknesses, but was in all points tempted as we are, yet without sin" (Heb. 4:15 NKJV).

That is good news! Jesus knows what we are going through. He knows how we feel, how tired we become, and He understands the heartaches that not even the closest human friend can share. Just like that five-year-old guide, He says, "I will never leave you nor forsake you" (Heb. 13:5 NKJV).

## THE KEY THAT FREES GOD'S HANDS

Dependence is the key that frees God's hands to work for us. Without his sight, my friend was dependent upon the instruction of another, one who could see! This lesson was brought home very forcibly to me on one of the many flights I have to take as I travel to speaking engagements and seminars all over the world.

I have learned to appreciate the air-traffic controllers as never before. I am glad that they can see the big picture, all the dangers and obstacles on their radar screens. They are in charge, and the pilots merely carry out their instructions. But it's more than the technology. I am grateful for the very real concern that the individual controllers feel for the safety of those in their charge.

For example, as my flight made its final approach to the Salt Lake City International Airport, the controller had done his job and our flight, thanks to the controller's instructions and our pilot's skill, was lined perfectly with the runway. Nearer and nearer the ground came until at last we were less than three hundred feet over the earth. Suddenly the invisible hand of gravity pressed me down into my seat cushion as the aircraft accelerated and climbed steeply upward. What had happened?

The pilot informed us that the controller had noticed what the instrumentation had failed to register. The landing gears were not properly deployed. In spite of the delay while the crew rectified the problem, not a single passenger objected to the controller's warning. His skill had saved us from destruction.

But let someone suggest that God should direct our lives, that we should obey His warnings and trust His guidance so as to avoid destruction, and we become resentful, resistant, and fretful. The reason is clear: we do not feel our need or sense our danger or our need of direction. We don't come right out and say we don't need God's guidance. In fact, we usually confess our need of Him. Our actions, however, give lie to our confession.

It is becoming increasingly popular in Christian circles to have "a form of godliness but denying its power" (2 Tim. 3:5 NKJV). For example, the phrase "What would Jesus do?" has become a popular Christian cultural icon, displayed on everything from T-shirts to toys, from pens and plaques to posters. It has been the subject of sermons and youth groups.

It sounds so good. It seems so right, and yet it is most often humanism masquerading as Christianity. The human is asked in his great wisdom to decide how Jesus would react in any given situation of life. Don't get the wrong idea. I am not picking on sincere people but demonstrating how natural it is for us to depend upon ourselves even in our attempts to explain spiritual truths. I know I've been in the same situations and done the same things.

Jesus Himself told us how He decided what to do or not to do when He said, "I do not seek My own will but the will of the Father who sent Me" (John 5:30 NKJV). He depended constantly on the Father's direction to give Him guidance.

I have often asked people what they would have done if they had been Jesus when He received the message that one of His best friends, Lazarus, was dying. You and I would have run off and healed our friend, but Jesus didn't do that. He stayed right where He was and let His friend die. You see, God had something wonderful planned for Lazarus, far more wonderful than being healed of his disease. If it had been us, rather than Jesus, we would have made a mess of those plans because we are not used to having God control our entire lives. We have not cultivated the spiritual sensitivity that Jesus had.

It may seem amazing to us that Jesus had to learn spiritual sensitivity, and yet the Bible assures us, "though He was a Son, *yet* He learned obedience" (Heb. 5:8 NKJV) and thus left us an example of how to overcome not in our own strength, but in God's.

The Lord has told us, "Cease ye from man, whose breath is in his nostrils" (Isa. 2:22 KJV). This means "Cease ye from every man," including our own great prideful reasoning and intellect. It means to cease from managing ourselves, to tune in to God and cultivate a daily spiritual sensitivity until it becomes a way of life.

Often an idea that seems reasonable in a theoretical setting is seen to be absurd when placed in a real-life setting. For instance, would you want to fly with a pilot who chose his actions based on what he thought the controller would tell him to do in a given situation, rather than inquiring of the controller? If we don't find this flight method very reassuring, why do we accept such practices in our religious lives? Probably it is because the whole of our religious experience is unbalanced.

We humans have the idea that a balanced life consists of God and us sharing the control of our lives, with God pulling upward and us pulling downward. This may be balance, but it leads nowhere. Hence, we must consider whether our religion has real-life application.

Does it lead us consistently upward? If not, then what we call "religion" is an unhappy life of constant pulling back and forth. Worse, it is a religion that permits our mental assent to truths to soothe our thinking and justify our deeds, while in reality we sit on the fence. It is the worst kind of deception, for we think we are walking the path to heaven, while we stay in exactly the same place, in the same condition, and just as fit for destruction as we were before we found this thing called "religion"!

Remember Rob, whom we met in the preceding chapter? Rob's religious experience needed to become practical. Simple, intellectual knowledge had not made him a new creature in Christ. As we saw, the first step for anyone desiring to possess a life-altering Christianity is to become "swift to hear" (James 1:19 NKJV). The willingness to really hear is the key that opens the door to effective communication in all our relationships, and its absence is the greatest hindrance.

## LEARNING TO LISTEN

Harold had been raised in what he described as a "cult type" religion. Coming of age, he rejected the doctrinal stances of the group in which he was raised, except for one thing: the group's simple country lifestyle. It was still dear to his heart, was his dream, so to speak.

At forty-five, Harold is typical of many Americans. He is in his second marriage and is raising three children from the two unions.

He and his second wife, Jennifer, age thirty, live in an affluent section of Connecticut just outside of New York City. Both are professionals and together they earn a great deal of money, but their lifestyle also incurs a lot of expenses.

Now in midlife, Harold is increasingly dissatisfied. He is making it in the world but is unfulfilled. As nominal Christians, he and Jennifer have bounced around from church to church over the last eight years.

Jennifer, while lower-key than her husband, is also searching, also dissatisfied with life. This is hardly surprising, for as a stepmother to two children from Harold's first marriage, she finds life often stressful. She and Harold went through a lot of difficult adjustments forming their blended family. Surely the future could only be better.

Now with a small child of her own, Jennifer has discovered that motherhood is the longing of her heart. If only she could stay home. If only she could have more children. If only economics didn't require her to work, then perhaps she could be happy.

The property sat in a neighboring state, consisting of more than one hundred acres of fields, woods, and a lake. The house was old but in great shape, as was the barn. It was the perfect country property, requiring only someone's dream to make it a reality. It was not expensive by Connecticut standards, and when Harold took a drive up to see it, he wrote an offer for it on the spot.

On the surface, it would seem this couple had compatible dreams. Surely this was a match made in heaven, but it was not to be. Very few wives would enjoy having their husbands choose to purchase a property without their approval, and Jennifer hadn't even seen the land yet. Then there were Harold's great dreams for the property, which included building a new house. Jennifer, ever practical, quickly realized that she was never going to be able to stay home with all those additional expenses.

Over the three months it took to close on the property, Jennifer tried to get Harold to understand her concerns, but he brushed them aside. Harold wasn't listening. He thought his wisdom was greater, his experience broader. Tension between them grew so severe that Jennifer refused to sign the purchase agreement.

Now, by any measure of judgment, there was a message in all this for Harold. But if he saw it, he refused to heed its warning. He felt he was entitled to his dream and nothing was going to stop him, so he purchased the property without her.

Many a wife has experienced this selective hearing. They may not have had their husbands buy property without them, but there are many ways we men can be insensitive to their concerns.

The changes came slowly and gradually. Jennifer wasn't sleeping well anymore. She was sullen and discontent at work. Her happiness at home was now only a bitter memory. For the first time anyone could remember, she began complaining about her husband, openly speculating on separating from him. Little things she used to overlook in love became insurmountable mountains.

Harold at last realized that his wounded wife was indeed becoming unresponsive to him and decided something was wrong. He decided work must be too stressful and encouraged her to look for another job. His inability to see his own selfishness and insensitivity, his unwillingness to hear, really hear his wife, confirmed in her heart the very worst she had thought of him.

Harold has yet to have his dream. Now they pay two mortgages, one for their Connecticut home and one for Harold's dream, while Jennifer's dream of quitting work and staying home turns to ashes upon the altar of stubborn pride and willful insensitivity. How long will they last this way? It's anybody's guess. Sad, isn't it? Surely we wouldn't be so insensitive. Or are we?

When I was courting Sally, I was very sensitive to her opinions, her comments, her thoughts and desires. She was constantly on my mind. I sat in class and wrote her name over and over on my notebooks and embellished it with hearts. It wasn't long after I married her though that I started to tune her out, to treat her like a convenience. What happened? I communicated only when it was convenient for me or if there was some sort of crisis, and bit by bit the marriage lost its zeal, its freshness. The very qualities that made the marriage living and vibrant and a joy to experience disappeared.

In taking Christ's name, Christians are in essence claiming to be married to Him. Far too many of us who have taken His name act just the way Harold and I did in our marriages. We either ignore the guidance of God and pursue our own goals, or we treat God as a convenience. We take time for Him when it is convenient, when we feel like it, then rush urgently to Him if there is a crisis.

My marriage improved only when the quality of the communication between Sally and me improved—or shall I say, when I truly learned to listen to her. This principle holds true in every relationship. Effective communication always begins with listening to the other party. My relationship with God has demonstrated this principle time and time again.

Listening to the voice of God is almost a lost art in today's society. So let's explore the avenues of communication between God and man.

## THE BIBLE, OUR ANCHOR

Most people think of the Bible when they think of God communicating with the human race. Certainly the Bible conveys to our minds an understanding of God and points out the pathway to obtaining a relationship with Him. "All Scripture is given by inspiration of God, and is profitable for doctrine, for reproof, for correction, for instruction in righteousness" (2 Tim. 3:16 NKJV).

Yet this same book of the Bible warns us that the Scriptures may be misunderstood or misapplied. "Study to shew thyself approved unto God, a workman that needeth not to be ashamed, rightly dividing the word of truth" (2 Tim. 2:15 KJV).

Volumes have been written on Bible study, and sometimes it can be confusing. Regardless of what you have or haven't tried in the past in your study, let me encourage you to leave other books and ideas and just come to God's Word with a heartfelt desire to have God provide you with practical guidance for the upcoming day. Come to the Scriptures as a sinner in need of salvation, and linger in God's presence. Be still and know that He is God (Ps. 46:10).

If you do this, the Bible will become more than sacred history, more than suggestions of how to live a holy life. Often we will hear the voice of God speaking to us personally from its pages.

True religion is the religion that transforms the entire life. It is an *experimental religion*. It is not just theory, but something we experiment with in a practical manner. Here the Bible shines forth in its brilliance. The Bible provides us an anchor, an infallible source against which we can test all our understandings. While the Bible is not the only way God speaks to us, it is the standard by which all others are judged.

## NATURE

Nature still points the way to her Creator. It was within the confines of the natural world that I learned to recognize the voice of God. When we eliminate the distractions of "civilized" society, our human minds are more apt to hear the voice of God. Even though it is scarred and distorted by sin, nature still reveals the wisdom and order of our God. Amid the glory and majesty of creation, we can sense our God's mighty power and feel our own inadequacy.

Yet the human mind can take even the most sublime of experiences and distort them to its own destruction. Charles Darwin traveled to a beautiful location, and there, surrounded by some of the most wonderful and unusual creatures of God's creation, he felt nature was speaking to him. But he did not bring the messages he felt he heard to the test of Scripture. Had he been willing to test his theories as God commands—"To the law and to the testimony! If they do not speak according to this word, it is because there is no light in them" (Isa. 8:20 NKJV)—then he would not have marched off into darkness and error, thinking he had found new and exciting light.

## PROVIDENTIAL LEADINGS

God also speaks to us through His providence in our lives. In His glorious pursuit for our affections, God arranges circumstances for our benefit. This is not some arbitrary action on His part to control us, but rather, like any parent, He works to alter circumstances so that His children, you and I, can make right choices.

Remember when I went to purchase the land, only to have it sold out from under me at the last minute? Was God directing me? It didn't feel like it at the time, but He was, and He will speak to you through the providence of life too.

There is another side to providential leadings. They are what I would call *fleeces*. In Judges 6 and 7, we are told the story of Gideon, whom God raised up to deliver His people. Gideon heard the Lord's instructions to him but was distrustful of his own abilities and talents, so he asked the Lord to confirm the directions given by the use of a piece of wool—a fleece.

> So Gideon said to God, "If You will save Israel by my hand as You have said—
>
> "look, I shall put a fleece of wool on the threshing floor; and if there is dew on the fleece only, and *it is* dry on all the ground, then I shall know that You will save Israel by my hand, as You have said."

And it was so. When he rose early the next morning and squeezed the fleece together, he wrung the dew out of the fleece, a bowlful of water.

Then Gideon said to God, "Do not be angry with me, but let me speak just once more: Let me test, I pray, just once more with the fleece; let it now be dry only on the fleece, but on all the ground let there be dew."

And God did so that night. It was dry on the fleece only, but there was dew on all the ground. (Judges 6:36–40 NKJV)

I have used fleeces in my experience. No, I have never laid wool on the ground. Maybe it would have been better if I had in some instances, but let me share one of my fleeces with you.

I was bow-hunting for deer soon after I became a Christian or, perhaps I should say, thought I had become a Christian. In any case, while I was hunting I heard the Lord speaking in the quiet recesses of my mind. That still, small voice said, "Put down your bow, Jim."

I knew this was the Lord, and I knew what He wanted me to do, but I was resistant. Almost defiantly, I told the Lord, "Well, if You want me to quit bow-hunting, bring someone to me with a thirty-five-millimeter camera and telephoto lens because I still want to go out in the woods. Oh, and Lord, they must bring it to me at half-price."

I felt pretty safe after this prayer. I had given the Lord a defiant fleece, an impossible task, the faithless plea of my unsurrendered heart. I would never pray such a prayer today! But that was where I was, back then.

Some time later, I got a phone call from a young man who was working in conjunction with our local church, selling Christian books door-to-door in the community. I greeted him warmly, and he asked if he could come over to see me. "Sure, come on over," I said.

He arrived shortly with a plain, brown cardboard box in his

hands. I was really curious by that point. He seemed to be in no hurry to inform me about the contents of the box. Finally, after he had comfortably seated himself, he calmly stated, "I have a story to tell you."

"Go ahead!" I blurted out.

"I was out selling books when I visited this one family. They were very interested in the complete set of Bible storybooks that I sell, you know, the ones for children. But they really couldn't afford them. They are about the most expensive books I sell, around three hundred dollars per set. I can't express to you how badly they wanted them. I could just see it in their eyes. It wasn't just the kids, Jim. The parents loved them too. I really wanted them to be able to buy my books, but I didn't know how to help them.

"At this point, the father made me an offer. He said, 'I have this camera. I just bought it a little bit ago. It's thirty-five-millimeter and has a telephoto lens. I paid over six hundred dollars for it, but I would trade you even up for the books.'"

My young friend paused. "Jim," he said in all seriousness, "I stood there not knowing what to say, and your name came to my mind. It was like a voice said as plain as day, 'Go ahead, and accept the deal. Jim will take the camera.' So I accepted the deal. Will you take the camera?"

Words cannot tell you how low I felt. The tears flowed down my cheeks as I wrote out that check because I knew I shouldn't have prayed that prayer, and yet the Lord understood. I got rid of the bow, and I have never hunted since.

## PROMPTINGS OF GOD

Probably the most misunderstood way in which God speaks to us is through impressions in our minds. Many people tell me, "I never hear God speak to me the way you say you hear Him speak to you!"

and I always respond, "Yes, you do! You just don't recognize God's still, small voice, or else you have so trained yourself to ignore His promptings that you don't hear them anymore."

Have you ever noticed that people who live near a train track don't even seem to discern the trains passing while the sound nearly deafens visitors? We can do the same thing with God. When we persistently ignore His promptings, they just blend into the background noise until they are almost unrecognizable.

I have a friend I'll call Arnold, to protect his privacy. He came to me after a sermon and said, "Jim, you say God speaks to you, but I've never heard Him talk to me the way He talks to you."

"He speaks to you, and you have heard Him," I said.

"I have?" he questioned skeptically.

"Sure you have," I encouraged him. "The last time you were in the grocery store and your eyes were drawn to the trashy gossip magazines or the ones with the scantily clad women on the front, what did the Lord say to you in your mind at that moment?"

I was fairly sure I knew the answer. Arnold may not have developed a relationship with the Lord that involved real communication, but I knew he claimed to be a Christian. And no one who is serious about being Christian can behold the images of the trash, trivia, and trouble displayed by the rich and famous or look on the sensual images of the latest fashions without the Lord prompting his thoughts, trying to protect his mind from such garbage.

"He said, 'Don't look!'" Arnold responded.

"What did you do?"

Silence.

"What did you do?" I asked again, but he wouldn't answer me. Oh, my friends, it is not that we can't hear God's voice, but that we have trained ourselves to be unresponsive to Him. I call it *selective hearing*. This is what causes us to think that we lead our lives without His guidance.

Now, not everything that pops into our heads is a prompting from the Lord. There are three areas from which these ideas spring. First, the Spirit of the Lord may prompt our thoughts. Second, our own flesh, which is made up of our passions, appetites, and desires, may be the source. Last of all, we live in a world that has been tempted into rebellion against God by the devil, and he is no less active in tempting us to sin than he was in any past generation. So how can we filter the thoughts that come to us and tell them apart?

We can and should bring promptings to the test of the Word of God. However, there are times when a prompting is neither inherently right nor wrong. An example of this was when the Lord asked me to move to the other side of the log I was cutting so that He could save my life. Morally, it was not wrong to cut on either side of the log, and there was no biblical principle involved against which I could test the prompting. What I did have was the beginnings of a familiarity with hearing the voice of God.

The more we listen to His voice, as with any friend, the more recognizable it will become. One rule of thumb I use to test a prompting is this: if the prompting asks me for self-denial—if it puts the needs and feelings of others before my own—I can be comfortable following it. These traits are the opposite of the sinful nature, the flesh I was born with, and they are not the character traits of Satan either.

We need to understand that the human mind, weak and failing as it is, remains the only medium through which God can communicate with any of us. Those seeking to communicate with the Sovereign of the universe should shun anything that weakens the functions of the mind. Certainly the use of mind-altering chemicals to achieve a so-called higher state of being should make one very skeptical about supposed messages received by individuals while in such states. God invites us to use the reasoning powers that He endowed us with in the following words: "'Come now, and let us reason together,' says the LORD" (Isa. 1:18 NKJV).

Many, many people are aware they receive messages in their thoughts that do not originate in themselves. The late singer, songwriter, and composer John Denver once explained it like this in his song "On the Wings of a Dream": "So I listen to the voices inside me. For I know they are there just to guide me."

Some Christians I talk to are uncomfortable with these promptings because they so closely resemble the messages received by those involved in the New Age movement. I have other friends who are actually in the New Age Movement, and their lifestyles closely resemble mine. They are debt-free. They live in beautiful wilderness homes. They eat a healthy diet. And yes, just like me, they hear promptings in their thoughts that they choose to obey.

However, they refuse to conduct their lives according to the Word of God and do not differentiate between the voices or acknowledge that these promptings could possibly be from the devil. The spirits giving them these promptings are demanding to the point they insist which shirts these people should wear. They have no freedom but serve the god of their thoughts. It so saddens me because they stand so close to and yet so far from truth.

No matter how much we desire God's guidance in our lives, there is a danger that we will approach God without subdued spirits willing to obey whatever He shows us to do. If we do not neutralize our own wills, then we tend to use our cherished ideas and goals as a standard by which to judge impressions and thoughts. When we have a thought that is in harmony with our preconceived ideas, it is not hard for us to assume that it must be a message from God.

Perhaps the largest hindrance to free and open communication with God is lack of exclusivity. God wants to go through every day with us as our constant Companion. He wants us to talk with Him throughout the day, depending upon His wisdom for guidance whether we are by ourselves, working, or visiting with friends.

Perhaps you may share an inclination I have to place God on the sidelines when I have a task to do. It is almost as if I say, "All right, Jesus, You sit over here. I'm going to get something accomplished."

## THE CURSE OF INDEPENDENCE

That is exactly what happened the day I heard my son's voice floating up the stairs. "Father, Mother wants to do a load of laundry, but the generator won't start!"

Fourteen little words were all it took to start a crisis in my life. I was at my desk studying God's Word when the call came. Surely no better time could come for a temptation than when one is studying the Bible—or could it? Can self even strive for control when one is studying the Scriptures? It surely can!

Immediately, irritated feelings rose up in my flesh because I didn't want to be interrupted. Besides, with the wind chill it was forty degrees below zero, and I didn't want to go out to the garage and wrestle with the cold piece of iron that refused to run.

Bundling up and walking out to the generator, I looked at it and could feel the battle raging in my heart. "You're not ready to deal with this yet," I could hear the Lord speaking in my thoughts. What did my strong German temper want to do? Have you ever kicked a cold piece of iron? The flesh doesn't care who gets hurt as long as it can vent its feelings and frustrations.

I walked back to the house and picked up a pen and paper to write the following: "Independence from God—the curse of Jim Hohnberger's life!"

Then I fell on my knees and prayed to the Lord until I felt subdued in my spirit. "Lord, this is our problem," I said. And it felt great to have Him carry the burden! "I don't know what's wrong with that machine, but You do, and I am going to depend on You to guide me." That felt even better! I was not going at the problem alone. Now the Lord of the universe was going to be at my side.

Returning to that troublesome machine, I felt the impression to check the points, but I checked the carburetor. After five cold minutes of fussing with the carburetor, I could find nothing wrong. The impression was still there about the points, but I checked the choke. I found nothing wrong there, so I moved on to the wiring. Still that impression didn't go away, and at last I gave in and checked the points, only to find a loose screw, which was shorting out the system.

I had gone to the Lord for help. I had even verbally placed my dependence upon Him. Then I ignored His leading. Talk about selective hearing. I had not learned the exclusivity required to make His voice, His input, supreme and all other voices—even my own "great" intellect—subordinate to Him.

## PRIORITIZING

Some years ago, Andrew made an old-fashioned wooden swing for Sally and me. It was a wonderful gift, and we have put it to use every day in what we like to call Swing Time. At noon, Sally and I put away our work and sit together. This is Sally's time to visit and share. Sometimes our talks are about deep and heartfelt concerns. Other times it may be a simple sharing of the events of the day. It is, however, scheduled time with my queen, time to listen, to really hear her. It is time I have learned to value greatly.

A friend came up to my house right when I was having Swing Time with Sally. We greeted him, and he explained his errand. "Are you in a hurry?" I asked.

"Well, I do have to get back to town, but I'm not in that big a rush," he responded.

"Great," I told him. "Why don't you go on into the house and help yourself to a book for a few minutes? I have an appointment with my wife."

He looked at me for a long minute and then went into the house.

My wife needed to know that she was more important to me than the unexpected visitor. This prioritizing is one of the keys to unlocking a vibrant communication with God as well as with our spouses. Satan works very hard to break down this communication in our marriages, for without this, they begin to die. Imagine how much more Satan wants to break the communication between the soul and God! And he'll use any means he can to do it.

He distracts our minds with everything from music to billboards, jamming our senses in the same manner that communist countries used to jam the *Voice of America* broadcasts. It takes concerted effort for us to retain a connection with God under the onslaught of noise and needless information in our modern society.

## THE ONE AND ONLY KEY

After a speaking engagement in Tennessee, my family traveled to the Nashville airport to fly on to our next appointment. Since we arrived a few minutes early, I decided to drop the family and our luggage at the departure entrance and then return the rental car rather than messing with the luggage on the rental company shuttle. Pulling up to the departure area, we were able to park right in front of the entrance. Usually, it is hard to park in these high-traffic areas, but that day we got the best spot imaginable.

As I pulled toward the curb, I felt the impression to take the keys with me, but I saw no reason to do that. After all, I could unlock the trunk with the little switch inside. But God had not given up on me, and again as I got out of the car, I felt the impression to roll down the window. But it was a cold morning, and I knew after unloading the luggage the warm car would feel good, so I ignored the impression.

After taking the luggage inside, I went back out to return the car to the rental agency and found all the doors on the idling 1998

Chevrolet locked, with the only key in the ignition. Immediately, I realized why the Lord had impressed me to take the keys, and I said, "Oh, Lord, I'm sorry!" My independence from God always spells T-R-O-U-B-L-E.

I have learned something about the airlines in all my travels: they don't wait for me if I am late. I was in big trouble because my flight was scheduled to leave in little more than an hour. I was also in trouble because you can't leave a car in this type of area more than a few minutes or the police will first ticket it, then tow it away. I ran back inside to get Andrew and had him stand by the car in case they wanted to tow it away, then I ran down to the rental car company.

The line at the car rental counter was huge. I knew my flight would leave before I ever got to the counter. Now that I was in trouble, I was motivated to listen, really listen to God's instructions. So I prayed silently, *Lord, what should I do?*

"Just go up to the counter and ask for the manager. Yes, the other people won't like it, and yes, you will be embarrassed, but it will be all right."

So I walked up to the counter and asked for the manager. He told me they had no spare keys, but that they could obtain one from the dealer. He quickly looked up the serial number for the car and phoned it to the dealer. The dealer sent a courier with the key and after meeting him, I ran back to the car only to find a policeman writing out a ticket while my son stood off to the side. He was very embarrassed about the whole situation and had not spoken up. I explained my problem to the policeman who, I'm thankful to say, had mercy.

As Andrew and I got back into the car, I wanted to ask him, "Why did you lock the car?" I would have, too, except that the Lord was speaking quite forcibly in my mind, telling me to be still. *But Lord,* I argued, *it's obvious he did it. I didn't do it, and he was the last one in the car. He probably just locked the doors out of force of habit.*

"Keep quiet, Jim. You'll find out down the road how it happened. Don't say words you will regret," the Lord replied.

Later, I told this story to my brother who explained, "Don't you know those new Chevy's have a timing device that locks the doors?" I didn't, and I was ever so grateful the Lord prevented me from falsely accusing my son.

Still, in looking back, there was a twinge of sadness, for I had spent the weekend preaching to others about being sensitive to the Spirit of the Lord speaking to us, and I had ignored His guidance and caused the whole problem with my selective hearing.

Often the things God asks us to do don't seem to make any sense. God didn't tell me I needed to take the key because the car would lock them inside if I didn't. Instead, He depends on us to trust that He knows what He is doing and, through faith in His love and wisdom, to obey His instructions. I call this *experimental religion* for the very reason that in each of these experiences I have learned lessons and grown in my understanding, even though I didn't listen perfectly. When I see the trouble I cause by not heeding His directions, it reinforces to my mind a familiarity with His still, small voice and a future determination to quickly obey His instructions. This process of learning to listen is the essence of experimental religion. It's learning what works and what doesn't.

## GOD CARES ABOUT OUR TROUBLES

I was plowing snow in the driveway one day while my family was working on various housekeeping tasks. After a while, Matthew felt impressed that I was taking longer than I should to plow the drive. *Maybe I should get on the snowmobile and check on him,* he said to himself. Now, Matthew also loves to drive the snowmobile, and because he likes it so much, he was fearful that this "impression" to go check on Father was simply an excuse for him to stop work and do something he enjoyed. Several times the impression came and several times he reasoned it away. Then I came in, all cold and snow-covered. The truck had broken down at the end of the driveway, and I had to walk back home through huge piles of snow.

Matthew then realized that the impression had come from God. But the experience wasn't a waste because he learned from it. How do I know? Well, on another trip, I was traveling with Sally and Andrew. Matthew was home alone. I just called to check in. "How's it going?" I asked.

"I'm learning to listen, Father." Then he told me this story. He had to take a client to see a property way up over a mountain pass. As he was leaving the house, he said that he felt a strong impression to bring a flashlight with him. *That's nonsense,* he told himself. *After all, I'm going to be home long before nightfall.* But the impression came again and, recognizing the voice of God, he went back into the house and got a flashlight.

"What time did you get home?" I asked him.

"Midnight."

A large spike—the kind used to connect logs into cabins—had found its way into one of his truck tires. His story thrilled my heart, for as a teenager he was learning lessons of dependence and spiritual sensitivity to God that I didn't even know about when I was thirty.

Would it be any easier for us to listen and obey the Lord if He did tell us the *why* behind His instruction? My own experience would indicate no.

When fall comes and freezing temperatures approach, one task that I must confess is not a favorite of mine must always be done: draining the water system in our guest cabin. The job isn't all that bad, but the crawl space under the cabin is dark, damp, and full of cobwebs. It's the kind of place you expect a spider or a mouse to jump out at you, and you wish you had some friend who would volunteer to do the job for you.

That cold fall day, I lifted up the trapdoor to the crawl space and climbed down under the cabin to drain the pipes. Needing more dexterity in my hands than I could get wearing my gloves, I set them on the ground beside me. Immediately I felt the impression to put them in my pocket because I might forget them. Now you can ask anyone who knows me: I have a wonderful memory. I don't forget things. So I reasoned away this impression and finished the job.

As I walked toward my house in the cold, I reached for my gloves, and you know where they were, don't you? "Oh, no! I forgot my gloves under the cabin," I wailed. I had no choice but to retrace my steps and retrieve them. In this instance, the Lord had prompted my mind, even warning me of what might happen, but the extra knowledge still did not affect my response to His instruction. I thought I knew better.

It was no great trial to retrace my steps, but it does illustrate how much God cares about even the little annoyances of life. This simple, almost trivial problem showed me only more how prone I am to do things my way and taught me to be more distrustful of my wisdom and self-reliance. God often works in small and simple ways to prepare us for greater temptations in the future.

Isn't that the way any loving parent would try and teach lessons: by allowing his child opportunity to fail when the consequences are minor? Unlike my New Age friends, I didn't have to fear when I ignored God's guidance. He was there to help me learn and grow from the experience and go on with Him.

In the end, we will be faced with a choice of obedience to God's promptings. We must make that decision based on a living faith as well as knowledge. As we experiment with practical religion, allowing God increasing control in our lives, then we will find ourselves learning more and more to recognize and trust His voice.

Just like me, you will have instances when you ignore His guidance and make a mess of things. But God does not abandon us when we do this, and if we are willing, He can teach us valuable lessons from these errors. So experiment with God, lean more and more of your weight on Him, leap out in faith, and trust His guidance.

If you do this, you will find Him not only an infallible Guide, but the best of friends to travel life's pathways with, both in this world and in the world to come.

*Chapter Eight*

# OUR GREATEST ENEMY

He must increase, but I must decrease.
*John 3:30* NKJV

WILLIAM MURPHY WAS an attractive, powerful man. Only forty, he was already an executive in a huge, international corporation. For the last week, however, he had been contemplating something other than mergers and contracts. He was forced to consider his own mortality.

It began at dinner with a dull, persistent ache in his jaw. Nausea soon followed, washing over him in waves. He told his wife he wasn't feeling well and wanted to leave the restaurant for home. Then he collapsed on the floor.

Paramedics found him to have a potentially fatal heart rhythm but managed to stabilize him. He regained consciousness in the emergency room and spent a week in a blur of tests and procedures. The diagnosis? Major heart attack. Worse yet, his cardiac catheterization revealed severe blockage in another artery. So he was scheduled for a procedure to open the blockage. That would not only prevent another heart attack but would hopefully save him from coronary bypass surgery.

Fortunately, the procedure went smoothly, and he was transferred to the post-procedure unit where his wife awaited his arrival. The cardiologist soon joined them with several "before and after" pictures in his hand. Using the pictures to demonstrate, the physician explained that the 95 percent occlusion of the blood vessel had been reduced to a less than 5 percent residual blockage. As good as that was, the specialist had bad news to share also.

He said, "Your lipids—that is, your cholesterol, the fats in your bloodstream—are still grossly elevated, with total readings more than twice the maximal normal. Worse for you is that the ratio of helpful to harmful fats is poor. You need to be on a cholesterol-reducing medication.

"I've also asked dietary to come and see you due to the fact that you need to be on a strict diet until these levels drop. In about six months, we will reevaluate the diet based on the decrease seen by then. Once you have recovered, I want you in a cardiac rehabilitation program.

"Finally, you have absolutely smoked your last cigarette. With any luck, we can prevent this blockage from recurring."

His pep talk over, the doctor answered a couple of questions and exited the room, saying, "I'll see you tomorrow."

William waited until the cardiologist was gone, turned to his wife, and said decisively, "I won't live like that!"

For a week, he had contemplated with sober thoughts the possibility of dying. Now that the specter of death had retreated under the onslaught of modern medicine, this otherwise intelligent, rational man was unwilling to take the steps necessary for his long-term survival.

Everyone thought that Bill's smoking, his diet, his high-stress job, his executive lifestyle, and his family history were to blame for his condition. In the end, these risk factors were not the enemy he needed to guard against. In truth, Bill's greatest enemy had already fought and conquered him. His own self-will was unwilling to sacrifice, unwilling to die. Desire was stronger than reason and appetite stronger than intellect.

When William dies at an early age, his death certificate will read "death as a result of natural causes." But in truth, Bill will have been murdered, slain by his own stubborn self-will.

When I moved to the wilderness, I was a lot like William. My spiritual life was in intensive care, in need of resuscitation. I thought I would escape from a number of enemies in the mountains—risk factors, if you will. I had thought that the worldly influences of the media were the enemy. I thought that the ministers who taught falsehood from the pulpit were the enemy. I thought that the cares and business of the fast-lane, workaday world were my enemy. I thought all these things were saboteurs that prevented me from living the Christian life.

And I was right. These things are enemies, and they do hinder the development of true Christianity. As much as possible, we should eliminate them from our lives so we can minimize their influence.

Unfortunately, I had the idea that battling the influence of these enemies was what constituted the spiritual warfare in my life. It wasn't until after I moved to the wilderness that I discovered that even in the most ideal environment I could imagine, I was still the same person who had left Wisconsin. I arrived to do battle with my sins only to find those sins were nothing more than symptoms of my real problem. Let me tell you, it was a bitter pill to swallow when I realized that the real problem, the real enemy, the real risk factor I faced was *me!*

I was the problem! My individual sins were just the inevitable fruit of self being in control of my life. It is here that oh so many who earnestly hope and desire to be Christians fail. God must have my whole heart—that merely represents all my choices surrendered to Him. He is not interested in having some of my choices or even most of my choices; He wants all. The key to living the Spirit-filled life is laying down all to the lordship of Jesus Christ. "No man can serve two masters," Jesus said. Why? "For either he will hate the one, and love the other; or else he will hold to the one, and despise the other" (Matt. 6:24 KJV).

## NO MORE GIRLFRIENDS

When I married Sally, I agreed to give up all my previous girl-friends. I gave all my affections to her. I relinquished all my former interests. I died to my old life of singleness. Now if I had tried to have a marriage with Sally while at the same time carrying on an affair with a previous girlfriend, what would have happened to my relationship with Sally? You know, don't you? We wouldn't have stayed married very long, would we? Suppose I excused my behavior and declared, "But I'm still married to her. She's my wife. I'm committed to her." It's a pretty ridiculous idea even to contemplate.

Yet, this is exactly what happens with most Christians. They try to hang onto their former loves while embracing Christ. At the same time, they indignantly denounce anyone who would dare question their commitment to Christ as unloving and judgmental. After all, they are good people. They do good things. They are born again, or so they claim.

The example of the rich young ruler was included in the Bible for a reason. He was a good man and a leader. Today many would look at him and say he was born again. But he wanted to be married to Christ while having an affair with self. He didn't want to leave his former girl-friend for Christ. So many miss the vital lesson of this story. It was not the fact that this man had great riches that kept him from Christ, but rather that he wanted to manage his life, his riches, himself.

At least six times in Scripture, Christ referred to His cross as ours. The terms Christ offers for discipleship are very clear. "If any man will come after me, let him deny himself, and take up his cross daily, and follow me" (Luke 9:23 KJV). Both the church and individual Christians have a poor understanding of death to self.

It is not a onetime death but a daily dying to my will and my way. This death occurs as I willingly allow the substitution of Another's (God's) will and way, no matter how crucifying this substitution is to my wishes or desires. It is when we willingly choose to give up the right to manage self that we are truly God's.

This was Christ's experience when He prayed, "Not my will, but thine, be done" (Luke 22:42 KJV). That I might gain this experience was God's goal from that very first day He launched that glorious pursuit for my life. In traditional Western courtship, a woman is not won to a man until she bears his name. In the taking of his name, she pledges her willingness to surrender not just her finances, her life goals, or even her privacy, but also the most intimate areas of her being. She is going to give her very self to the one she loves.

Few who claim to be Christians desire this depth of intimacy and surrender to God. Fewer still have obtained it. Why? Because it is a process, and the modern church has completely lost sight of this fact.

## A PROCESS

When you start dating someone, you do not begin at the altar. Instead you set out to win her affections. God does the same with us. Gradually feelings develop for the other person. At first she has a little place in your heart, and you are willing to give a little of yourself for her. Then this special person becomes more important to you, and your willingness to give of yourself for her increases and continues to grow until you are merged into one flesh after marriage.

Our relationship with God is the same way. It's a gradual process, leading us to a marriage that is a merging of two into one.

The worldly view of Christianity popular today confuses this process so badly that the minute one expresses any interest in

Christ, he is considered to be a Christian. The Bible often speaks of the church being married to Christ. In light of that, let's use the analogy of courtship to gain a better understanding of the process of becoming a true Christian.

In life, the condition before marriage is singleness. We'll call it Stage 1. This person is usually open to consider another state. In Christianity, that state of singleness would be a life lived apart from God. The self rules his own life and does not consult God. The willingness to consider Christ having a role in one's life varies with the individual.

Then in Stage 2, someone comes along and expresses an interest in the person. Something she says or does awakens a response within, and he is willing to let her into his life, maybe just a little bit. So it is with God. He shows us His love and care, and His interest creates a desire in us to let Him have a little part of our lives. Many think they have become Christians at this stage, but it is only the beginning.

The interest expressed in Stage 2 creates affection that grows into a courtship—Stage 3. In this stage, the desire to join lives is born. Usually an engagement is announced. Yet the individual is still single. He still has control and can still change his mind. Nothing is written in stone, so to speak.

For the person considering Christ, the experience is very similar. God continues to woo us to Himself. The individual learns lessons of dependence and trust in God. He begins to learn to surrender the will to God. He develops the desire to make God a lifelong partner. Yet self is still in control, and a fully surrendered "marriage" has not taken place.

The last step, Stage 4, is marriage. When both individuals are willing to forsake all others and put each other's needs above their own, the marriage takes place. They blend their wills to become one flesh. It's a daily commitment to another person.

When the human whom the love of God has pursued and won chooses to fully surrender to God, it is at that point he or she becomes a Christian and is in essence "married." In this marriage, self has to die, and no one or nothing else can hold a higher place in the heart than God. Only after full surrender does the taking of Christ's name have real meaning.

To maintain and deepen this commitment is the new Christian's challenge, yet freedom of choice still remains. A married person chooses to be unfaithful. The difference between changing one's mind in Stages 3 and 4 is that in Stage 3, the commitment has never been made. God never removes the person's right to change his mind. He never forces us to have a relationship with Him. Instead He constantly draws us with love.

"Jim, are you really saying that one is not a Christian until he reaches Stage 4?" you might ask.

My answer is yes, no one is a Christian on the basis of profession or knowledge. We are Christians only when we place our total dependence upon God. Anything else is a combination of the human and divine and dooms its adherents to a knowledge of duty while robbing them of the power to obey.

"But, Jim," you might say, "it seems the whole Christian world holds a different standard. I mean, all of us understand what you're saying on a theoretical level, but you've got to meet people where they are. Perhaps this is all very well and good on an intellectual level, but is this really practical?"

It is very practical. Come with me through a typical day and see if this experience isn't what you have longed for all your life.

## A VITAL YET PRACTICAL CONNECTION

When you're a realtor, every time the phone rings, it is both an opportunity and a challenge. It was no different late one afternoon when Dan called me.

"I want a second home up the North Fork Valley, and I was told at the office that you were the best person to talk to. What makes you so special?"

"Dan, I'm not sure I can answer that question because it is probably different for each person. I have been very fortunate to live in the wilderness for many years, and I know the properties well. My background is as a business owner, and perhaps that enables me to connect with clients, many of whom are businessmen, but most of all, I would like to think people refer clients because I take a sincere interest in their needs and not just my own financial benefit. With this in mind, tell me about yourself, your family, your expectations, and your aims and goals for the property."

We chatted for some time, and it became clear that he was well qualified to purchase a second home, but he did not want an isolated wilderness home. He and his wife liked neighbors and wanted people with whom they could socialize. Immediately I thought of a lovely wilderness lake where the homes, while not crowded by any means, would provide a sense of community. When I asked him when we could schedule a time to look at the property, he told me he was in the area only one more day, and it would have to be the next morning.

I had planned to do some paperwork that morning for a closing coming up at the end of the week, but I wanted to help Dan, so I offered to take him to the property the next morning as long as he was willing to meet me by nine o'clock.

By the time I got off the phone with Dan, I had just a few minutes to copy some property information for him before I left with my family on an evening bike ride. I don't know why, but I just don't naturally enjoy cycling. I do it because my boys enjoy it, and I enjoy them. That night, however, was different. The route Andrew chose for us was challenging, and dodging around trees and rocks took my mind off the day's activities. I could just feel my mind relaxing while my body worked to keep up with the boys.

We were all getting hot and tired as we worked up a hill, and I decided to take my water bottle and splash Andrew as I passed him at the top of the hill. So I put forth extra effort to catch up with him. He was slowing down as I crested the hill, and when I reached out the bottle to squirt him, he turned. I didn't know the trail turned, and I found myself headed down a steep incline that terminated in a very muddy puddle. I splashed through, the water fanning out in all directions, and felt incredibly cool and refreshed. Amazingly, I found my unexpected detour brought me down the hill much faster than the others, and when they saw me ahead of them, they pulled out their bottles and chased me all the way home, each of us laughing and giggling until we could hardly ride. When I got home, I needed a shower.

The excursion left me relaxed and ready for bed. Our fun time had created a happy, warm feeling in all of us that lasted as we had worship that evening and went to bed. As I walked by my desk, the paperwork called out to me. Remembering my morning appointment, I was tempted to sit down and work just a little longer. I have learned that the next day begins at nine o'clock the night before. That's because if I am not in bed at nine, I will not get up early enough to spend the time I need with God.

This time is important to me. I am passionate about it because I have found that God is passionate about me! It is a wonderful time when I can come to Him as my very best Friend and am empowered or filled with His grace for the coming day. I spend lots of time every morning in prayer and quiet contemplation of His Word, asking my heavenly Father to prepare me for the struggles that lie ahead. Not only does He know what's coming, but He has also planned my escape. God's faithfulness to deliver me is a constant revelation to my poor, dull senses of just how much He loves me.

I don't study for information or doctrine during this time. I approach God's Word as a sinner desperately needing salvation. I come to catch a glimpse of one far more holy and powerful than I am. When one looks at a majestic mountain or the grandeur of the Grand Canyon, the normal reaction is one of awe and wonder. Unless drugs or alcohol dulls your senses, you realize the puniness, the insignificance of man. This is the vision I want to gain of God every morning, a vision that makes me realize just how weak and powerless I am.

If through communion with God I can come from my time with Him with a sense of my own need, it makes me willing to take Him with me throughout my day because I know that without Him, I can do nothing.

So many who have tried to have morning devotional time find it a powerless experience. They say their prayers and maybe read the Bible or a devotional book, but they never find a vital, living connection with the Source of power. Because this is a new experience, we are not intuitively prepared to obtain communion with the Almighty. Humans learn most things by observation and imitation, yet devotional time is by definition an intimate and private time—not something we are likely ever to see another person engage in—so how do we learn to make it profitable?

Perhaps the most important thing I can share from my own experience is to linger in God's presence. Just because He doesn't seem to be communicating with us does not mean this time is unprofitable. The number-one reason we fail to connect with God in our private time is that we have not allowed enough time to let go of the burdens of life, to realize our need, and to become quiet and teachable. Seek after God the way a drowning man seeks rescue. Long not for knowledge about religion or the Bible, but rather seek for a knowledge of God Himself, for He says, "'Then I will give them a heart to know Me, that I am the LORD; and they shall be My people, and I will be their God, for they shall return to Me with their whole heart" (Jer. 24:7 NKJV). Upon leaving this quiet time with God, I always find an opportunity for self to rise. After breakfast this particular morning, I hurried to finish my household jobs because

Dan was coming to pick me up. We have divided the household tasks in such a way that my wife doesn't have to bear the whole burden of housework. The boys make their beds and help with both the cooking and the cleaning. I am in charge of planning family worship, making our bed, chopping and bringing in wood, and sweeping the porches. I also provide additional help where needed to make things run smoothly.

As I passed my son's room, I noticed his bed wasn't made yet and felt impressed that I should make it for him. I was in a hurry and tried to discount the impression. After all, it was his job, and I wanted him to learn to be responsible. But the impression came again and with it a reminder that I had promised God that I would do whatever He told me to do that day. So I went over and made my son's bed and headed off to complete my own chores.

Among my tasks that morning was to chop wood for the stove. Because we live way out in the wilderness, we both heat and cook with wood. I like chopping wood and don't really find it to be a chore. However, due to the very nature of the work, it is easy to let the mind wander, and I found myself thinking about a friend who had a disagreement with me. The tendency in my thoughts was to see all his faults and justify my position. The same familiar voice that had communed with me that very morning again called to my heart.

"Jim, you need to pray for your brother, not enter into self-justification."

"Well, Lord, what should I pray for?" You see, self had risen almost imperceptibly and now I was hesitant.

"Jim, I want you to pray that you can do something for your friend who disagrees with you. I want you to pray that you can do something that will cost you of your time, your talents, or your money."

After a moment of struggle right there at the chopping block, I chose to surrender. Self was put to death, and I prayed that prayer. And wouldn't you know, within a few weeks, God answered that prayer and gave me an opportunity to do something for this man.

It occurred to me that while he was away from his place traveling, a lot of snow would have accumulated at his house, which is no fun when you arrive home tired and just want to relax. I felt the Lord had brought this to my mind and wanted me to do something about it. I went to his house and did all the snow removal, a task that certainly cost me of my time. He never knew who had helped him out, but with every shovel my heart was drawn out toward this man and my thoughts purified of my resentful feelings.

That's where battles are won or lost, my friends, in the thoughts. I didn't know it then, but I had several more battles to face in my thoughts that day.

As I finished my tasks, I noticed my client had just pulled up to the house, and I greeted him at the door. I stepped into the laundry area where my jacket hung and what do you suppose I saw? There sat a load of wash my wife had done. It was just waiting to be hung on the line.

"Jim, I want you to hang out those clothes for your wife."

"But it's not on my chore list, Lord, and Dan is waiting. Besides, those are my wife's clothes."

"Jim, I want you to hang those clothes out on the line for your wife. Oh, and Jim—they're your clothes too."

Right then and there, I had a battle to fight in my thoughts. Should I obey? If I did, what would this man think of me, especially after I had made him come early? Would it be fair to make him wait while I hung them out? The conflict happened so fast. I am happy to say I chose to surrender my thoughts and wisdom to an all-knowing God. I invited Dan in and offered him a glass of water. "I'll be just a minute," I said as I headed out the door with the laundry basket.

At the clothesline, a new battle raged. I wanted to do a "hurry up and get it done" job. Was I willing to do a good job and shake out all the wrinkles just as my wife would have done? The biblical principle is whatever your hand finds to do, do it with all your might (Col. 3:23). My flesh wanted to rise up and control me. It would have been so easy to justify self and think, *She ought to be thankful I'm hanging it out at all.* The Lord was with me in that seemingly insignificant time of need, encouraging me to submit and obey. Deep down, I knew from bitter personal experience that this was the only way to true happiness.

As I carefully hung each item, I became aware of eyes boring into my back. My backward glance confirmed just what I suspected. Dan was standing at the window, glass of water in hand, staring at me in disbelief. It really only took a few minutes before I was able to climb in my friend's car, and we were on our way.

"Jim, why were *you* hanging up your wife's laundry?" he asked.

"First of all," I responded, "it's not *my wife's* laundry. It's *our* laundry. Secondly, God told me to do it." Funny, I had just had that same conversation with God.

"What do you mean, 'God told you to do it'?" he asked.

"I mean God spoke to me in my thoughts and told me to hang out the wash," I told him. My battle opened up a theme of conversation, which continued the whole morning. I had no idea that by obeying God's promptings, I would have an opportunity to explain spiritual things to Dan, but I did. By the time we returned to my home in late morning, this man was my friend and had decided he wanted this kind of a walk with God too.

You see, God knows just what is needed to reach every person. The problem is getting each of us to cooperate with Him.

Bidding my friend good-bye, I walked into the house anticipating that I would be able to spend some time in Bible study and prayer. However, as soon as I went in, I could just sense that my wife was struggling. She had been homeschooling the boys. It was her day to cook the midday meal, and the whole load of wash I had hung out was dry and waiting to be ironed.

"Help your wife, Jim," said that old familiar voice.

"But, Lord, I had planned to study." Can self even be involved in Bible study? It sure can, especially when something else comes up that crosses our plans. Each time the decision to let self die comes, it comes a little closer to home. For me, ironing is a fate worse than death. I don't like to iron clothes, not even a little bit. I do iron clothes, but I do it out of what I would call principle.

Starting on the load of clothes, I ironed a couple of shirts, and then I came to one of my wife's blouses, one with lots of little pleats on the front. They aren't easy to iron in the first place, but to iron them perfectly, you know, the way Sally would, required the sustaining power of God. By the time I finished the blouse, Sally left her meal preparations to come over to look at it. It passed her inspection! I couldn't believe it! Praise God! I felt triumphant, and for the first time, I found some joy in ironing the clothes.

I was mostly done with the load of ironing when Sally called us to eat. It was a lovely meal. She made all my favorites: peas, corn, wild rice, and homemade biscuits. Little did I know that my next battle with self was just moments away. As we sat down to eat, I noticed a small container of home-canned tomatoes on the table. Now, that may not seem important to you, but I *love* home-canned tomatoes. I like to pour them over things like rice or even corn, but there was a problem, and I knew it at first glance. Only one serving remained in the jar, and to my side sat my eldest son, who loves the tomatoes every bit as much as I do, if not more.

I bowed my head to say the prayer, but even as I prayed, my flesh screamed out to me. "Grab them quick! Get them before Matthew does. You deserve them. After all, you paid for them." Have you ever heard your flesh speak that way to you?

I don't even need to tell you what the Lord told me to do, do I? And again I faced a choice. So I sat there and watched Matthew eat those tomatoes, and you know something, I survived. Isn't that amazing? To listen to the voice of my flesh and the longing of my appetite, you would have thought that my life itself depended on those tomatoes.

The meal over, my sons went to work on the dishes. Sally took over the dregs of the ironing, and I found myself with some free time, so I sat down in the recliner with my Bible. A slight noise announced the fall of something plastic, and sure enough, the cap to the spray starch had fallen at Sally's feet.

"Pick that cap up for your wife, Jim," whispered the familiar voice of my constant Companion. At first, I wanted to argue and say, "It's right there at her feet. All she has to do is pick it up. I am reclined and comfortable. Why do I have to get it?" I'm thankful the Lord doesn't enter into such controversies with us. He simply lays out the path of duty, and it is up to us to follow without excuse or complaint.

I set the Bible aside and returned the recliner to its upright position. I walked over and picked up the cap, then set it on the ironing board and returned to my chair. As I sat down, I met Sally's loving gaze. That look told me everything. I knew she understood the self-denial it required for me to get up out of that chair. The knowledge of her sympathy and the fact that my simple kindness had deepened her love for me more than repaid my effort.

Toward the end of the evening, my son came to me. I could see something had deeply moved him, but I had no idea what it was. He hesitated, then spoke. "I saw you make my bed this morning," he began. "All day long, I waited for you to take credit for it, but you never did. Can we talk about the Christian walk, the one you're having?"

## LIBERTY TO CHOOSE

So now you have met my worst enemy—me! We each have an enemy with whom to do battle. What are you going to choose to do with your enemy—yourself? It is easy to laugh over the things we do to ourselves, but in the final analysis, it is no laughing matter. In allowing self to remain and rule in our lives, we are killing ourselves just as surely as one who commits suicide.

I spent much of my own life seeking *my* way and looking to make *myself* happy. Let me tell you, it was a miserable existence! When we choose not to surrender self, not to allow that old carnal nature to die, then it is that all the conflict and discontent of life rises within us, ruining not only our enjoyment, but doing the same to all about us.

Within us lies the ability to choose whatever level of existence we want. The freedom to choose, the ability to exercise our will, is the greatest gift with which God has endowed the human race. Properly used, the human power of choice, in response to God's grace, connects us to the God of the universe, and through His power and direction, we will become a blessing to the world. Improperly used, the same power of choice will guide the human into actions that make the whole world shudder. Look back at history, examine the dictators, those whose very names have become synonymous with evil, and realize that in every case, it all began with a seemingly insignificant choice to have their own way.

# Chapter Nine

# DO YOU REALLY BELIEVE?

Lord, I believe; help my unbelief!
*Mark 9:24 NKJV*

ONE OF THE blessings of wilderness living is water of a wonderful quality. I felt I could make life easier at the cabin by installing a gravity-flow water system. This type of system will not work on every property, but if the elevations are correct, nothing is better in a wilderness setting. It requires no power, and there are no parts to break down.

Our property is one of those fortunate ones with a spring sitting about sixteen feet uphill and two thousand feet from our home. To have gravity-flow water, all we had to do was have a backhoe come and dig a deep trench below the frost line and lay over two thousand feet of pipe.

Unfortunately, after laying the two-inch pipe, I found that I needed to go to town for some pipe fittings. An early-morning trip to town would give me time to buy the fittings and install them before the backhoe operator arrived at 9:00 AM to start backfilling the trenches.

Rising at my normal time of 4:30, I felt the pressure of the three-hour round-trip to town, and the inclination was to rush through my personal time with the Lord. "You understand, Lord. I usually spend time with You, but this morning I have things to do."

The Lord impressed my mind with this thought: "Jim, you need to spend time with Me and make sure you have a vital connection rather than a casual connection. Stay with Me until your flesh is subdued."

Surrendering my plan to the Lord, I stayed and had my personal time with Him. I left the house contemplating my subject of worship that morning, which was John 15:5: "I am the vine, ye are the branches" (KJV). I was thinking about the close and vital connection the branches have with the Vine as I drove toward town along the deserted North Fork Road.

Suddenly, a big mule deer leaped out of the ditch on the side of the road in front of me. There wasn't even time to hit the brakes before I hit him broadside at fifty miles an hour. There was a sickening thud of the impact accompanied by the sound of breaking glass and plastic. The hood accordioned, and the grill gave way. Steam rose from the radiator. Shreds of the grill punctured its surface. The fan's clickety-clack joined the hiss of the radiator to make a very forlorn sound. The radiator had been pushed all the way back to the engine block. Leaving a small trail of broken parts, I came to a stop at the side of the road.

The last thing I felt like doing at that point was abiding in the Vine. Yet as I sat there still holding onto the wheel, I could hear that soft, still voice that never ceases to call for our attention. "Jim, you need Me right now. Do you believe I am still with you and can work out this problem for you?"

"Lord, it doesn't feel like it. I mean, my plans to obtain the parts seem as good as lost. The backhoe man is coming, and I'm not going to be there to meet him. My truck is destroyed. The fan is going clickety-clack. The steam is rising. Not only will I not be home at 9 AM, I will be lucky to make it home tonight. No, Lord, it doesn't feel like You're with me right now." I wanted to get out and examine the damage, but as usual, God had other plans for me.

"Jim, do you remember that breakfast your wife packed for you?"

"You have got to be kidding! My truck is smashed, and You want me to sit here and eat?"

"Jim, if you don't eat now, you won't have time later. Your blood sugar will drop. You'll get weak and irritable. You need to get out the granola and eat it slowly and quietly."

"Eat it slowly? Why, Lord, I can't even do that at home, let alone here in my smashed truck!"

"Just trust Me, Jim."

"But Lord—"

"Chew slowly, Jim."

So I sat there and ate slowly, or at least I tried to. At the end of twenty minutes, I was done with the granola. I was wondering if an angel was going to appear, but none showed up.

"Jim, you know that apple your wife packed for you?"

"Lord," I exclaimed, "the apple too?"

So I sat there, slowly eating my apple. As I finished the apple, I saw a U.S. Forest Service truck coming up the road from the other direction. As the truck rolled to a stop, I gratefully realized I knew the driver.

"Well," he said as he pulled up to my window, "you're in quite a fix here."

"I sure am," I agreed.

"Listen," he responded, "I have a dispatcher radiophone here in the truck. Do you want me to call a wrecker for you?"

"Yes, please."

After he placed the call, he went on his way, and I was left to contemplate the fact that someone else had come along the deserted road and that he had a radiophone in the truck. This was long before the days of common cellular phones, and radiophones were rare.

I felt impressed that I should get out of the truck and pick up all the glass and parts I had scattered over the road. That way my trial wouldn't inconvenience anyone else, but first I decided to take care of the deer. I could already see the deer was dead. It lay in the road, broken, a thin stream of blood flowing from its once-noble head. I felt terrible, and tears came to my eyes over the waste of such a wonderful animal. I just couldn't allow it to be hit again even in death, so I got hold of the legs and dragged the poor creature to the roadside. Later, as I picked up the last of the parts, the wrecker from town came and proceeded to hook up my truck.

"Where do you want me to take it?" the driver asked.

I remembered that I had sold some property to a nice man who owned a body shop, so I gave the driver his name. As I rode along in the cab of the wrecker, I realized I was going to have to get some type of rental car, and again the temptation was to worry over the details. As strange as it might sound for a former insurance agent, I had no rental insurance, and I felt irritation rising in my heart. This was going to cost me money and lots of it!

"What happened, Jim?" asked the body shop owner who recognized me as I walked in the door.

"I hit a deer," I responded.

"Well, I must say you did a good job of it," he said, surveying the damage with an experienced eye. Looking up at me, he asked, "How are you going to get around?"

"I don't know," I said.

"Well, I do," he responded. "This car-rental place was just in here the other day, and they gave me a bunch of coupons for free rentals. They're yours!"

"Thank You, Lord" was all I could breathe to myself. Just then the tow-truck driver stuck his head in the office and offered me a ride to the car-rental agency, which I gladly accepted.

As I climbed back into the wrecker, I couldn't help but think of how God had made provision for me. But I know many people, all equally loved by God, who've had similar problems that didn't work out so perfectly. Why? God is never surprised by our changing circumstances or problems. He has foreseen and made provision for each and every one of them. But often we miss such provision because we do not consult Him, or we simply do not realize His provision because we are so wrapped up in our problems.

Too often, I have found from my own experience that I have a problem and start down the pathway of expecting the Lord to show me a solution, and when no such solution is quickly forthcoming, I take matters into my own hands. God has a solution, but He never forces our will. If we want to be in charge, if we want to be in control, He does not force us to follow His way.

This was my struggle as I ate breakfast in my damaged truck. Before I understood this, I would have looked around and started hiking to the nearest house, finding my own solution in my own way. Such a decision is not inherently wrong or sinful, but it is not dependence upon divine wisdom. As I got out at the rental company, I realized I had learned a lot about what it meant to abide in the Vine that morning. I thanked the driver and got a car, the parts, and even made it back home in time to get the job done.

At some point, everyone who claims to believe in the Lord must confront himself with the question, *Do I really believe?* Did I really believe that I was the branch abiding in the Vine that morning? The branch does not spend any time worrying over whether the Vine is going to take care of its needs. It simply concentrates on growing. None of my worries that morning accomplished anything. The Lord worked out all the details, and He did it without any help from me.

Christ spoke to the people of His day about worthless worries in these words: "Therefore do not worry, saying, 'What shall we eat?' or 'What shall we drink?' or 'What shall we wear?' . . . For your heavenly Father knows that you need all these things. But seek first the kingdom of God and His righteousness, and all these things shall be added to you" (Matt. 6:31–33 NKJV).

Do we really believe? I wonder.

## Grizzly!

As I shared earlier, there are many bears in our area. I rejected the idea of arming myself for protection. Instead I decided to depend upon the Lord to defend me and to warn me when there was danger. Many people viewed this attitude of dependence upon God as presumption, and even I knew that sometime, someplace, this plan of mine was going to be put to the test. Then and only then would I have the opportunity to confirm whether I really believed in my God.

The opportunity came, but not exactly in the way or at the time I expected it to. I wish I could say to the Lord, "At eleven o'clock tomorrow morning, I will be ready to be tested on patience." But it doesn't work that way. We must always be ready to give an answer for the faith that lies within us (1 Pet. 3:15).

The ravens were carrying on in the woods. This usually means some type of animal has died. My boys were concerned that one of the deer we fed treats to by hand might have been the victim, so they asked if they could go exploring to find out. I not only gave them permission to go but agreed to go along too.

Now, young boys do not always want to move at the same pace as their father, and I let them run on ahead toward where the ravens were crying. The trail split into two different paths paralleling each other. The boys took one, and I unknowingly took the other.

The idea that there might be a grizzly bear on the carcass never occurred to me. It had, however, occurred to a bear. Fortunately, my two boys were quite young and excited. They made sufficient noise so that the bear heard them coming and decided to leave with all possible haste, right down the trail I was walking.

The bear and I met face-to-face at close range. The bear reared up on its haunches, growling and snarling. Grizzlies seem to hold the opinion that if you aren't looking for trouble, you should keep your distance, and if you want trouble, they will be only too happy to oblige.

I had always known that someday this would happen. Secretly, I had wondered how I would react in that moment. Would I turn tail and run or drop to the fetal position and cover my head as all the experts on bear attack instructed people to do? Maybe I would try to climb a tree or fall to my knees in desperation. None of these thoughts came to mind.

As I stood eye to eye with that most feared beast of the wilderness, I sensed not fear but Someone stronger standing by my side. In almost a casual gesture, I reached out and broke off a small twig from the branch in front of me and said, "Lord, he's all Yours!"

Friends find it hard to believe that my pulse wasn't racing wildly, but it's true. There was no panicked rush of adrenaline or sweat on my brow, just a quiet assurance that I was in the hand of my constant Friend and Companion. I knew that the Sovereign of the universe was my Shield and Protector.

One of my favorite promises in all the Scripture is "'I will never leave you nor forsake you.' So we may *boldly* say: 'The LORD is my *helper; I will not fear.* What can man do to me?'" (Heb. 13:5–6 NKJV, emphasis mine).

Still gazing at the bear—which seemed to have materialized out of nowhere—I worried that my boys might come down the path looking for me. I wanted to yell and warn them to stay where they were. But this would be inviting disaster for me. Yell at a black bear, and it will usually run. Yell at a grizzly, and it will charge. My choice was easy—as a parent I had to protect my boys.

"Boys! Stay where you are!" I shouted. True to form, the grizzly dropped down to all fours and started to charge me when suddenly she wheeled about to look behind her. My boys were trained from the time they were little to come immediately when called. So when I called out "Boys," they didn't even wait to hear the rest, they simply came running.

It was their voices and the noise of breaking twigs and branches as they moved toward us that dissuaded the bear from charging. Soon my boys appeared on the other side of the bear, who was by this time both furious and desperate to escape these strange creatures who did not play by the usual rules. Taking a wide detour around me some thirty feet off into the woods, the bear returned to the trail behind me, all the while growling and sputtering, leaving us with no doubt about her feelings toward us. Then she turned and ran down the path.

Talk to anyone who lives in bear country. We did everything wrong you can do in a bear encounter, yet we had been protected due to the benevolence of a living God, who not only controls all the creatures of this world but walks by our side.

## Hold That Plane!

Not long ago, I had to fly to Akron, Ohio. From my local airport in Kalispell, Montana, there is no direct flight. All flights are routed through the airline hub at Salt Lake City. My flight to Salt Lake City was uneventful, and as I boarded the flight for Cincinnati, Ohio, and found my assigned seat, I had no idea things were about to go as wrong as they possibly could.

The captain announced there was a mechanical problem and that our flight would be delayed. Immediately, I prayed, "Lord, You know I have a connecting flight to Akron. Please help these men to resolve this problem quickly."

Instantly, I sensed this was going to be a trial. I had only forty-five minutes between my arrival in Cincinnati and my departure for Akron. I was scheduled to speak that evening, and if I missed the connecting flight, all those people would be kept waiting. So I prayed, "Lord, You know the needs of those people. Don't let the devil triumph. I know You can get this plane off with enough time to spare. Please, Lord, help these men get this plane off with time to spare!"

Twenty minutes passed, then thirty, then forty minutes, and then the captain announced that we would be taking off in five minutes. "Lord, forty-five minutes. I'll miss my flight. It will be departing as I arrive. There is no time to spare, not even one minute." As I poured my heart out to the Lord, He prompted my mind with these thoughts:

"Jim, do you believe I am with you?"

"Well—yes—I preach that."

"Do you believe, Jim? Do you really believe that I can hold that flight for you?"

"Yeesss," I said with a little trepidation, "I believe You can."

"Do you believe that I will?"

Now that's a much deeper question, isn't it? "Yes, I do."

"Will you do all you can in order to make that flight?"

"Yes, Lord."

"Then I will hold that flight for you."

So I asked a passing flight attendant, "Can you have the pilot call ahead and hold that plane for me?"

"Sir," she said gently, "we have more than four hundred people on this plane. We can't be doing that for four hundred passengers."

"But," I explained, "it's not that Grandma and Grandpa are waiting for me at the airport. There is a whole auditorium full of people, and I'm the speaker, and if I'm not there—"

"I'm sorry, sir."

I thought maybe she was just hard to get along with, or I had approached the subject wrong, so I tried another flight attendant and got exactly the same response. So I changed tactics and asked something that would seem to be very selfish, but I wasn't asking it for myself but rather on behalf of the poor people who would be waiting for me in that auditorium.

"Ma'am, could I be the first person out that door when we come to the terminal?"

She looked at me as if to say, "My, but you're rather self-centered, aren't you?" After I shared my dilemma with her, she was very obliging. "Yes, as soon as the plane comes to a halt, come by this door, and I'll stand here with you. When that door opens, *go!*"

*Great,* I said to myself. *God is with me, and the airline people are cooperating. God is going to hold that plane.*

Cincinnati has a huge airport with many terminal buildings and an endless maze of gates. I asked the flight attendant who was helping me exactly where I had to go in the giant complex to catch my flight. It was three terminals away! So I took my sweater off and put it over my arm. I knew this was going to be a rather hot experience. With the sweater and the briefcase, I was at the door when it opened.

Several years ago, there was a commercial showing a football player running through the airport, leaping over baggage and dodging other passengers. Remember that one? Well, that was me! I was jumping and dodging and running. I was perspiring when I arrived at my gate and said, "Where's the flight?"

Nobody was there except the attendant who said, "Sir, it left five minutes ago."

"But God said He was going to hold it for me!" I blurted out.

She looked at me. I mean, she really looked at me. I wish you could have seen her expression. "Sir?" she said, questioningly.

"Ma'am, you have to call the pilot and bring that plane back in because I have to be on that flight. God assured me that flight would be held." I could see the plane as it was being taxied out. "Can't you get a truck and put me up on a ladder? I mean, there it is! You have to get me on it!" But she wouldn't do it.

She looked at me like, *What in the world has gotten into this guy?* I knew in my mind that God was the God of all flesh, and that there was nothing too hard for Him. I had believed that! Did I really hear God speak to me? Did He really care about getting me to that appointment? I walked away from the attendant's podium and sat down in one of the chairs in the departure area, bowed my head, and prayed, "But Lord, You said—"

The Lord said to me, "Jim, do you *really* believe that I am the God of all flesh? Do you really believe that I can bring that plane in even now if I choose to?"

I said, "Lord, I . . . I don't know. I'm not sure. I don't know, I thought I did. I did everything I could, just as You asked me to. I believed, Lord, but the evidence is before my eyes . . . Yes, I believe, Lord, but help Thou my unbelief."

As I was sitting there in that chair, wrestling and struggling to come to terms with what had just happened, the attendant tapped me on the shoulder. She said, "Sir." I looked up at her, and she continued, "I don't understand it, but the plane is coming back to the gate."

"Praise God!" I said, leaping to my feet. "What happened?"

"I don't know," she said.

"You have to find out!" I implored her.

"I will, I will. I want to know too!"

She called the plane and then called me over to explain. It seemed that the man who was directing the plane—you know, that person who is always standing there with the cone-shaped flashlights—noticed that the front tire was frayed, and he ordered it back in for a tire change. This was what was going on while I sat in my chair with my head bowed, and God was asking me, "Do you really believe, Jim?"

I hope to meet that attendant someday because I have to ask her some questions. I was so excited about getting on that flight that I didn't say anything at the time, but I wanted to ask her, "Do you believe in my God?" I want to ask her because I could tell from the look in her eye she thought I was just kind of "different." Someday I want to ask her, but I may never have the opportunity. So I want to ask you: do you really believe in my God?

Friends, God delivered me from the grizzly bear. He provided everything I needed when my truck was destroyed. He brought the airplane back in for me. Do you believe He is just that personal of a God for you? Do you think He can deliver you from all of your problems? Do you really believe that God has the solution for every difficulty or perplexity you may face?

No, you don't! And that is why we have problems in our homes with our children, with our spouses, and in our churches. Why don't we see that hand of God in our lives like this? Where is the problem? Do you think the problem lies with God?

The problem is us! We are so busy finding our own solutions in our own wisdom that we never go to the God of the whole universe who has the solution. We don't go to the Lord and say, "Lord, I need You. Please take me, step-by-step, out of my troubles."

"Why," I asked the Lord, "couldn't You have had the plane there at the gate? I would have believed!"

"Because it is in the darkest hour that I shine the most, Jim. Did you have a role to play? Yes, but remember Zechariah 4:6 says, "'Not by might nor by power, but by My Spirit,'" says the LORD of hosts' (NKJV). Jim, it is so you will understand that none of your talking to the flight attendants, none of your fantastic running through the airport, none of your trying to convince the attendant to put you up in a ladder did you any good. I had you do those things to see if you would obey and cooperate with Me, but there's no power in anything you can do. It's all in Me."

God often allows us to come to the darkest hour so that He may deliver us, to remind us that He is the great God of the universe. When we seek God continually in all things, then we can experience His keeping. The Christian life is made up not only of surrender to His leading but also a receiving of His power. "But as many as received him, to them gave he power to become the sons of God" (John 1:12 KJV).

God wants to give His children power to deliver them from all their difficulties, trials, and perplexities. Isaiah 58:11 says, "The LORD will guide you continually" (NKJV). Don't you want that? God wants to manage your life, your affairs. Will you agree to be led?

Then you will have a personal experience with God. It may not involve an airplane, but I guarantee that you will have a story to tell of God delivering you from your troubles. Then you can tell others how God has delivered you that they may be believers too. That is why God allows me to have these experiences.

So, let me ask you again: *do you really believe in my God?*

*Chapter Ten*

# GOD AS MY ALL IN ALL

Not that we are sufficient of ourselves to think of anything
as being from ourselves, but our sufficiency is from God.
*2 Corinthians 3:5 NKJV*

"JIM, WILL YOU come to the Realtors' meeting next month and
share the secrets of your success with the other agents?" the owner
of the real estate agency asked.

"I'd be delighted to," I responded and went happily on my way.
I was flattered. After all, when I started my wilderness real estate
practice, a number of these same professional realtors had expressed
the opinion that I would starve up in the mountains. Now, I was
the number-one realtor in their ranks, thanks partly to the fact that
nobody else worked my valley. That meant I got all the listings and
made all the sales.

I had been in sales all my life, and I felt I understood a thing or
two about the relationship between buyers and sellers. Certainly, I
could share the methods and techniques that had helped to make
my practice prosperous.

All was well until my quiet time with the Lord the next morning.

The Lord asked me a question to which I had no ready answer: "Jim, are you going to tell those realtors the *real* reason for your success? Or are you simply going to share with them the part that your humanity has played in helping you succeed?"

"But Lord," I protested, wishing to avoid the trend of our conversation, "they don't want to know You—the Man behind my methods. They are just interested in my techniques."

I knew that the businessmen and women were not expecting any type of spiritual emphasis, and a battle raged in my mind. What would happen if I got up and told the real secret of my success? I could picture them asking me to leave right in the middle of my speech. At the very least, even if they didn't throw me out, I knew they wouldn't understand where I was coming from, and it was likely that all my fellow realtors would reject me.

"No, Lord. I just can't do that!" But the impression wouldn't go away. I had to deal with it, and at last I told the Lord that I would tell them the *real* secret to my success.

The day arrived, and as I stood in the podium and looked out on those individuals gathered to hear my secrets, I trembled. I wondered how they would receive my message. I sensed that my dependence had to be upon God.

This was not the first time in my life that I found myself battling a mixture of fear and dependence on God in my heart. Before we go on, let me share about the time I was . . .

## Out of Air!

The steady intake of air sounded strangely muted under the waters of the quarry. Sally, my dive partner, looked trim and professional in spite of her missing buoyancy compensator. It was a look that belied our limited experience. Our compensators, while ordered, had not arrived. Newly certified, we had returned to the quarry to practice our skills.

For that day's dive, we were wearing old-style life vests with a mouthpiece through which we could add air as needed. Both of us wore weight belts, fins, masks, and tanks, which were, of course, equipped with regulators containing gauges and mouthpieces.

Sally and I had performed our open water certification dives at this same quarry. We had spent a lot of time in class learning how to regulate buoyancy. The human body, when the lungs are filled with air, is naturally buoyant. This means that when immersed underwater, it will tend to rise toward the surface. For a diver to remain under the water, he must use one of two methods. The first is propulsion. The diver uses his own efforts to exert the force necessary to keep his body under the surface in exactly the same way the child in a swimming pool does when he ducks under the water to retrieve an object from the bottom of the pool.

Scuba divers whose very objective is to spend time under the surface of the water have no desire to spend all their time and effort maintaining a certain depth. Hence, they favor the other option: they wear weights to overwhelm their natural buoyancy, allowing them to slip beneath the surface with ease.

However, not just any old amount of weight will do. Divers work hard to strike a balance between the weight's tendency to pull them down and natural buoyancy's wish to pull them up. Buoyancy compensators allow divers to increase or decrease their buoyancy by adding air as needed to the vest-like device. Theoretically, the old-style, air-filled life vests, that Sally and I wore, worked the same way.

I had studied the principles of diving and knew the physics involved. Reaching the bottom of the quarry at the fifty-foot level, I found I was a little too negatively buoyant and was bouncing off the bottom, stirring up clouds of silt that obscured my vision and made the dive less enjoyable.

Remember, I knew the principles that regulated diving. Those principles told me that if I added some air to my vest, I would stay off the bottom. So I dropped the regulator, took the mouthpiece to the vest, and blew and blew. But for some reason, I was unable to get much air into the vest.

As I later learned, the reason was the depth. The deeper you go under the water, the more pressure is exerted on every square inch of your body. Hence, I couldn't apply enough force from my lungs to overcome the pressure surrounding the life vest, so no air went into it. Another complication is that when you blow your air out at that depth with the surrounding pressure, you really blow your air out! Therefore, when I gave up on the vest and reached for my regulator, I was in real need of another breath.

But I couldn't find my regulator. As an amateur, I didn't fully realize that it had drifted behind me. Another amateur mistake had been to place my tank too high, preventing me from being able to look behind myself and find it. I was ready to panic.

I had only a few choices. I could take off my gear and find my regulator, but I was not very adept at such maneuvers. I could go off and look for Sally, or any other diver, although no one was in clear view at the moment. I knew that any diver—even one who had never seen me before—would share his air with me. Last of all, I could make a free ascent up to where I knew there was air. I opted to make a free ascent.

This option had another problem. A diver can rise no faster than his bubbles if he is to prevent the "bends," a very painful, sometimes life-threatening condition where there is too much nitrogen in the blood. I had no air left in my lungs to blow out any bubbles, so I picked a pace that seemed about right and began to plan for the what-ifs.

What if I couldn't make it to the surface before I passed out from lack of air? This was a real possibility! My body was screaming for oxygen at that point. I placed one hand on the release clip for my belt and the other on the control for my carbon dioxide cartridge. My vest was equipped with the cartridge to inflate it when it was serving its normal purpose of being a life vest. I knew that inflating it fully would draw me to the surface, and even if I was unconscious, it would hold me up out of the water. Dropping the weight belt would allow the vest to pop me to the surface even faster, but I wasn't going to risk the bends unless I absolutely had to.

About halfway up, it happened! Involuntarily, I tried to breathe, and there was only water. I knew what a drowning person must feel. I pulled with both hands, and as the vest inflated and the belt dropped away, I popped up to the surface, coughing, sputtering, and gagging. Floating on the surface, I was thankful for the sea of air that surrounded me. I had been in a hostile environment, one in which man was never intended to live. While in that inhospitable location, my full dependence was upon my breathing apparatus. When I lost hold of my breathing apparatus, the environment in which I found myself began a coldly unmerciful attempt to destroy me.

So it is with you, my friends. All of us live in a world filled with sin, an environment in which God never intended us to live. So we must place our full dependence upon God—our breathing apparatus, so to speak. When we lose sight of our dependence, we find ourselves adrift in the sea of sin, an ocean just as full of peril as the deepest sea.

There is a problem. You and I know it from experience. Our whole existence seems almost by design to hinder this type of moment-by-moment dependence upon God. Life is very bold! All sorts of thoughts and feelings leap out and demand our attention. The seductive beauty of the advertisers' models captivate our interest. The decibels and the hypnotic beat of modern music insist that we listen. The pull of our own flesh, its demands and its wishes, come at us with almost overwhelming intensity. Unless we remain in a state of dependence, it is little wonder we find ourselves letting go of God.

Most of us have an inbred desire for friend-to-friend communication with God. But in reality, no matter what we desire, we usually end up communicating with ourselves. We mull over thoughts and fret about what might happen in the future. This proclivity to analyze our situation often results in our failing to engage in any sort of meaningful dependence upon God. Because we have thought it out, and, in so doing, drawn our own conclusions, we are led all too frequently to ignore the quiet voice of God speaking through our consciences.

We have so thought out our situations, so planned them, that we become convinced that we have no other options. When Jesus suggests another course of action to us, we tune Him out, ignore His help, and flounder on all alone. He longs to help us but cannot because we are unwilling.

The biblical history of God's people is, to a greater or lesser degree, played out in each of our lives. The Jewish nation refused God's guidance and killed the messengers He sent them. We refuse His leadership, then blame those who bring us a message of rebuke. How often might the words Christ spoke of Jerusalem be applied to us: "Thou that killest the prophets, and stonest them which are sent unto thee, how often would I have gathered thy children together, even as a hen gathereth her chickens under her wings, and ye would not! Behold, your house is left unto you desolate" (Matt. 23:37–38 KJV).

As I travel the globe, I stay in an awful lot of desolate houses— the homes of people who sincerely believe they are Christians. I meet so many people who are prisoners of their thoughts. Often they are living in the past, consumed by yesterday's wrongs. They spend their days in self-justification. These individuals are often the very first to admit they made mistakes but seem blind to the fact that they have learned nothing from them. Their past errors resulted from dependence upon themselves, and the pattern continues to this day, as their thoughts continue to rule in their lives. Let's look at one such situation.

## PRISONERS OF OUR THOUGHTS

A woman approached me, following one of my speaking engagements. I watched her mournful figure trudge up the aisle. Her eyes downcast, she seemed burdened with the weight of the world.

"Brother Hohnberger," she began, "I want to talk to you about my husband." She appeared to be alone. I hadn't noticed any men nearby that appeared to be connected with her. Already I was feeling impressed that whatever the woman's problems were, her husband was not the source of them.

"May I ask you a question?" I inquired. She nodded, although she seemed disconcerted by this unexpected query. "Ma'am, how long have you been thinking evil thoughts about your husband?"

She just stared at me, so I continued, "I can see it all over your face. I bet you have never had freedom in your thoughts toward your husband. Have you?"

"No," she admitted. She had not.

"Now, you want me to talk to you about your husband. He is not even here. If you want to talk about your husband, bring him here, but I can't do it without him. I can, however, tell you how you may have freedom in your thoughts, how you can have a right attitude toward him for the first time in your married life. If you want to talk to me about that, I'll be glad to help you."

This woman had dwelt on negative thoughts until it had affected her whole facial expression. She looked sour and unhappy because she was sour and unhappy. She wanted to speak of her husband's faults and how to get him to reform. The very best way to get a spouse interested in reformation is for you to have a reformation in your own life. Why would her husband want anything to do with this woman's religion when she was obviously miserable?

If our thoughts are not under Christ's control, we deceive ourselves if we think we are abiding in Him. Our thoughts and our feelings make up the character we possess, and, therefore, it is essential that Christ control them. If we are willing to submit our thoughts to Him, then they will no longer control us. But it is more than just a surrendering of our thoughts. More specifically, it is a decided willingness to yield to our Lord's judgment when He calls for us to surrender *any* thought to Him.

I used to think that such a situation would make me miserable, would reduce me to the level of a robot. Nevertheless, when I tried it, I found there is a special freedom that comes with constant dependence. Things suddenly seem to work out for me in a manner that I could have never dreamed, and I find joy in life precisely because someone else is in control. Let me illustrate.

### Apologize? For What?

After a weekend speaking engagement, we found ourselves only a day's drive from Sally's mother. Realizing this ahead of time, we had planned our itinerary to include a rental car and some time to drive down and visit her.

Most of the time, airport rentals are straightforward with a certain rate and unlimited mileage. This particular location didn't offer unlimited mileage, and I had negotiated a rate, including the type of mileage I needed, with the company's national reservations number.

Arriving at the rental counter, I found three other customers in front of me. The poor woman at the counter appeared new and struggled through the computer system while the customers complained about the delays.

At last, the others had been cared for, and it was my turn. I was the last customer, and I could just sense that the clerk was tired. Other customers had been rude, and when she pulled up my reservation, everything about it was wrong!

"Jim, apologize to this woman for being a thorn in her side," the Lord said.

"Apologize? Lord, for what? I haven't done anything to her that's been improper." This is the tendency toward self-justification that so often we allow to push God aside as we try to run our own lives. I could rationalize my feelings. I was tired too. I had a long drive in front of me, and what my flesh wanted was for this woman to get herself together and treat me right.

"Jim, I want you to apologize not because of what you have done, but for the sake of this woman."

I still wasn't fully convinced, but I turned to the woman and said, "I'm sorry to be a thorn in your side."

She looked at me in shock for a moment, then responded, "Sir, I . . . er . . . I mean, you're not a thorn in my side. It has just been one of those days."

"Do you think we can work this problem out?" I asked gently.

"Sir, I'm sure we can!"

And she did although it required a call to the national reservations number and two calls to her boss at home on a Sunday. I left an hour later with the right car and the right rate. "I know it's been a rough day, but hang on to Jesus," I said as I left the counter. "He has the strength to get you through."

I'll never forget her response. She smiled an endearing smile and said, "Thank you so much for being so understanding!"

It required an hour of time that I wanted to spend driving to my destination, but in choosing self-denial, I left that airport on top of the world! I knew that God had used me to touch another person's heart and encourage her!

I don't naturally possess the wisdom to know what to say to defuse a hard situation like that. But I'm learning that if I will keep my dependence upon God, lives can be touched. And in the process, I am transformed and awed by the wisdom and mercy of my Father who cared so much for this woman and her hard day that He wanted to use me to speak words of sympathy to her.

## JIM, YOU NEED TO GO!

Step back in time with me for just a moment, to a certain winter evening more than ten years ago, when I was first learning dependence upon God's wisdom. It was well after five, and the weak winter sun had set. Darkness settled upon the wilderness except for the faint illumination of the moon. "Father, let's go cross-country skiing!" Matthew exclaimed as I lay back in the recliner.

Remember what I said earlier about the immediate problems of life tending to stomp out our dependence upon God? Well, my flesh wanted to say something like this: *What do you mean? I've already had my shower, and the last thing in the world I want to do is go out and get all sweated up again skiing. I'm comfortable, and I don't want to!*

"Matthew, I've already had my shower . . ." I began.

"Jim, have you asked Me what you should do?"

"Well, no, Lord, but . . ."

"Jim, you need to go cross-country skiing with your son."

I had learned that the Christian life is about choices, and I made mine. "Let's go!" I told Matthew. I wish you could have seen his face. You see, my previous response about my shower had already told him what my choice was, and he had started to turn away with the attitude of "I knew you wouldn't go." Now his face lit up, and he ran to get ready.

The Christian life is one of living by principle rather than feeling, which is a good thing because my feelings were unsettled as Matthew led the way uphill. I was working and sweating, and the comfort of the warm, dry cabin with my feet up in the recliner was now just a memory. "Lord, is this just to humble me?" I prayed. There was no answer.

At last, we started downward, and I took the lead. As we entered an area of thick evergreens, the moonlight was almost fully blocked out, and an oppressive darkness hung in the air. I felt impressed to stop in that eerie spot and wait for Matthew. As he drew up beside me, I felt impressed to ask, "Son, if you were here right now, and I wasn't with you, how would you feel?"

The light was extremely bad, but even so, I could see the answer on his face. "Thank You, Lord," I breathed. You see, I didn't know, hadn't even suspected, but Matthew's words confirmed my impression.

"Father, I would be scared to death!"

My oldest son, Matthew, was scared of the dark!

God knew it all along, but I didn't. Only by obeying God and going skiing with my son was I able to become aware of the problem and help him, through the grace of God, to overcome this fear. It wasn't exactly unknown to me. I could sympathize. I had been scared of the dark my whole life until I became a Christian.

Countless people go around like Matthew, fearful that some unknown monster is going to attack them. The Christian need not have such fears. Fear is an element of evil, and when we are tempted to be fearful, we need to ask the Lord to deliver us from those feelings. In the same way, the Christian must surrender other feelings such as hurt, anger, or bitterness to the Lord.

I talked to Matthew about this and shared how I had overcome these fears: after I surrendered them to God, I looked for opportunities to confront those lies of Satan and prove them false. Matthew grasped the concept and earnestly desired deliverance from these wrong feelings. Soon, I saw him exercising the principles.

For example, his mother asked him to take something to the garage one evening, and while he hesitated, he agreed to do it with a flashlight. On his way back to the house, he heard the voice of God prompting him with a quiet "Why don't you try it without the flashlight?" He did, and his delight knew no bounds when he saw he could walk in the dark and not be afraid.

It took several months of lots of little incidents and practice sessions like this. Step-by-step, Matthew vanquished his fear of the dark. Please don't misunderstand the point. It wasn't that Matthew overcame this fear on his own or even with our help. Rather, Matthew gained the victory through God's grace over Satan, who had been harassing him with these thoughts of fear. He learned to turn the feelings of fear over to Jesus and leave them there.

## GOD IS MY TRAVEL AGENT

One day, I had to make one of those flights I dread. It was a four-flight trip, and a good portion of it on an airline I don't normally fly. I had to fly from Montana, change planes at Salt Lake City, and at last in Cincinnati, Ohio, make a connection to Asheville, North Carolina. My flight was late arriving in Salt Lake City, and my connecting flight was leaving just as I arrived. It was going to be a while before I could get on another flight, so I sat down to rest.

I had prayed that the Lord would, through His providence, work something out so I could make my other connections on time and not inconvenience those who were going to pick me up for my speaking engagement, but it appeared that this was not to be.

Glancing over from my seat in the waiting area, I noticed the sign-up booth for that particular airline's frequent-flyer program. The Lord prompted me with this thought: "Go sign up."

*I don't feel like it. I missed my flight, and I don't fly this airline enough to make it worthwhile.* God often does things like this. He asks us to do things that seem to our human wisdom and reasoning not to make any sense. His real reason is cloaked. In any case, I got out of my chair and headed over to the counter, for I was learning to let God be all, and in all, for me.

After telling the attendant I wanted to sign up for the frequent-flyer program, she asked for my ticket. This was a little unusual, but I handed it over. "When are you going to get a flight out?" she asked. I told her what I had been told about the time for the next flight, and she responded, "Sir, we've got a flight leaving right now, and I can get you on it." I was not only on time for my connection, I was actually early!

Now why did God use the guise of signing me up for the frequent-flyer program to help me make my fight? Think what my reaction might have been if He had said, "Jim, go to the frequent-flyer desk. The attendant there will get you on an earlier flight." You know, don't you? That's right. I would have argued with God. After all, it is ridiculous to think that the frequent-flyer attendant had better flight information than those at the ticket counter.

God is so kind that He often saves us from ourselves by holding back from our knowledge that which might hinder us. Therefore, God sometimes asks us to do something under a pretense that we understand and will act on, when in reality, He who can see the end from the beginning is, in His wisdom, ordering events for our benefit.

What a wonderful God we serve! It is a shame that so few who claim to be Christians actually know Him. Astonishingly, most churches these days do not promote Christ but themselves. The churches, religious schools, and colleges have built themselves into mighty bureaucratic institutions that have forgotten the very purpose of their founding.

Today the church, by and large, returns converts to itself rather than to God. Funds become the lifeblood of all such empires, and all that hinders the free flow of funds is shunned. Therefore, we sit, satisfied to convince the members they have been born again and are saved rather than teaching them to make God all, and in all, in their lives. It is a fearful record of neglect that the Christian church, all the Christian churches, must one day face.

Christ's life and ministry clearly rebuked this building up of the institution, this linking of people to a church rather than to God. Christ did not oppose the Jewish church in His day but was more concerned that the individual gain a living, vibrant connection with Him rather than hold membership in the church (Hosea 10:1; Ezekiel 34:1–16; Matthew 15:14; and Matthew 23:1–38).

## KNOCKING KNEES

In many ways, today's ministers have the same dilemma I had as I stood before those realtors. Do we share the popular, expected message, or do we share with our hearers that which has a chance of transforming their lives, even at the risk of unpopularity or critical comment?

I began with my presentation on good sales techniques and the relationship between buyers and sellers. Then, I said, "If you follow the steps I have outlined for you this afternoon, you will find success in your practice, but not the kind of success I have had. It is kind of like my son's cookie recipe. Everyone loves his cookies, and he gives the basic recipe out to anyone who asks, but when they go home and make the cookies, they complain that they just don't come out as good as his do. This is because my son uses a secret ingredient in his cookies that no one else duplicates.

"My son pours love into every cookie. He prays that the Lord will bless his efforts, and God does because while other people use exactly the same recipe, they do not get results that are as tasty as his.

"Friends, there is a secret ingredient to my success as a realtor as well. The secret to my real estate sales is a living connection with the Lord Jesus Christ, every moment of every day. God sends me my clients, He opens up new listings for me, He is in charge of all aspects of my business and personal life. I filter all things through Him, and this enables me to inquire of the Lord what is the best property for my client—after all, I know He brought them to me for a purpose. This enables me to put ambition and concern over my profit aside and tell some clients that this isn't the type of area they want to live in: 'I can tell your wife doesn't want to be this far from town. It is too remote.' I sometimes tell other clients that they are overextended: 'Sure, the bank would probably give you the loan, but they don't care for your happiness down the road. I do. Sell your other property before you buy.'

"Friends, my secret of success is that I am not their realtor, God is! He simply allows me to act as His representative. This is the secret to success available to any of you who wish it."

I had worried and fretted so much about their reaction, but at least 90 percent of those present thanked me for the presentation. They told me it brought back their childhood upbringing, and more than one observed, "What are you doing selling real estate? You ought to be a preacher!" Little did I realize how prophetic their words were.

So, what about you? I know you cannot enjoy living life the way you have been. It's hard to breathe without a breathing apparatus. Do you want to try to place your dependence upon God? Will you allow Him to be your all, and then make Him all in everything you do or think? He bids us, "Come unto me, all ye that labour and are heavy laden" (Matt. 11:28 KJV).

Come to the air. Come make Him your all. Paul said, "Put ye on the Lord Jesus Christ" (Rom. 13:14 KJV). He is your breathing regulator. He is the only thing that allows you to survive in this world of sin. And after you have put Him on, never let Him go!

# Chapter Eleven

# THE FOURTH PIVOTAL POINT

"How long will you falter between two opinions?
If the Lord is God, follow Him; but if Baal, follow him."
But the people answered him not a word.

*1 Kings 18:21 NKJV*

TEARS POURED FROM my eyes uncontrollably. The individual drops formed tiny rivers as they made their way down my cheeks and dropped onto the bed while other drops followed my nose until they splattered on my Bible. How long I sat this way, I'm not sure. Sally awoke and looked up at me. "Honey, why are you crying?" she asked.

*Where do I begin?* I wondered. *Do I start with the weekend's speaking engagement? Do I go back to the invitation? How can I explain it when Sally has unwittingly been involved from the very start?*

At last I decided to start at the very best place . . . the beginning! So I took a deep breath and began to tell the story of the fourth pivotal point.

*Webster's New World Dictionary* defines *pivotal* this way: "the thing on which something turns; the central, crucial, or critical point." That morning with Sally, I had definitely come to a decision that fulfilled that description. It was, in fact, one of several pivotal points in my life and the fourth one of which I was aware in my relationship with God.

When I first learned of the Word of God and saw that it was more than fables and prayers, I quickly reached the first pivotal point in my relationship with the Lord. If I accepted His Word as the sole guide of my life and was serious about applying the truths it contained to my life, significant changes in the way I lived my life would take place. Was I willing to let God have that much rule in my life?

I decided that I would make those changes and accept His revealed will for my life. I found this changed the way I viewed myself and my family. I quit smoking and drinking because I saw that my body was the temple of God. Christ had died for me and purchased me at the price of His own life, therefore I was not my own to do with as I pleased.

As I learned more about the Bible, I tried to share, and my zeal—well-meaning though it was—drove a wedge of prejudice between my *extended* family and myself. The choice to try to follow God's Word dramatically altered the course of my life. Hence, my first pivotal point was accepting the Word of God as the absolute authority in my life. Sally had been right there beside me making these same hard choices.

My second pivotal point came when my understanding of God's Word led me to join a church different from the one in which I had been raised. Some people seem to switch denominations as most of us change shirts, but for me this was an earth-shattering step. I knew that I should not take true religion lightly. It was a hard thing for me to realize that even though sincere parents had trained me and raised me with certain beliefs, those facts alone do not make a religion a practical, life-changing force.

The third pivotal point was when God convinced me that we needed to move to the wilderness and become truly converted. This was a struggle because so many we had thought were solid Christians opposed our plans and worked hard to convince us that we were mistaken. Now we understand beyond all doubt that we made the right choice.

It could be argued that every time you and I face a choice, we are at a pivotal point, and to some degree that is true. But the pivotal points of which I speak are the far-reaching, life-altering choices that change the course of our personal histories.

When Moses sent twelve spies into the land of Canaan, ten of them chose to present a discouraging report before the people. Only two were hopeful. The nation was at a pivotal point! Their choice to turn away, to become discouraged, cost that entire generation the opportunity to enjoy the land of promise.

## THE FOURTH PIVOTAL POINT

After several years in the wilderness, I suddenly felt myself caught up in a pivotal decision. We had found just about everything that we had gone to the wilderness to obtain. We had come to truly know God and were growing ever closer to Him. Learning to subdue self and remain surrendered to God yielded spectacular results.

We moved from being married to having real *marriage*! The family changed into a real *family*! My wilderness real estate practice took off and provided a great income for our family. We were out of debt, and I was working only three days a week. We kept the influences of the outside world to a minimum, and even in conjunction with my work, we went to town no more than twice a month.

We had it made! We were living our dream!

At the moment of success, the Lord said, "Jim, I want you to put down the real estate. I want you to work for Me in a full-time ministry. The focus of that ministry will be restoring lives, marriages, and families."

I remember saying to God, "Lord, I can't!" And I was right. In my own strength, I couldn't minister for the Lord, but that wasn't fully what I intended. Instead my comment revealed my real feelings. "I have life made, Lord," I said. "You are asking too much!" I would have to leave my beloved wilderness home for days, even weeks, at a time to do His work. Full-time ministry was a total unknown with no apparent security.

As I thought about it, I struggled to decide. I looked at the life of Moses, who was in line to be king, to be pharaoh, when God asked him to leave it all behind. Then there were Peter and the other fishermen Jesus called to follow Him. He asked them to follow a poor and unrecognized preacher. Those choices were pivotal points in their lives. Nothing would ever be the same, no matter what they decided. And I quickly realized that this call to ministry was a pivotal point for me as well.

I wanted to talk to Sally, but I was afraid to talk to her because I knew what her answer would be. She would remind me how God had led us so far, and she would say He would not leave us now. Hers was a simple faith, but for me this was a huge struggle. I was responsible for providing for my family, and I had no confidence I could do so in a ministry.

Worse still, I loved the life I was currently living and had no desire to change anything! It was only my confidence in Sally's willingness to do whatever God asked that allowed me to feel I could work through this privately. So she was an active participant although she knew it not.

Dear reader, you, too, have pivotal issues in your life today. I don't know what God is asking of you, but you do, and the Holy Spirit does. There is something God is asking you to deal with. He wants you to choose to go deeper with Him.

I pray that the Holy Spirit will place this decision at the forefront of your thoughts as you read. I pray that God will give you no peace and no rest until you are surrendered fully to Him. I surely had no peace as I strove to come to terms with this unexpected call to ministry.

There I was in the wilderness, enjoying the fruit of the lifestyle God had called us to, and I had to decide what would become of this standoff between my soul and God. The rich young ruler in the Bible had a standoff with God, and it cost him everything. Now I had to choose if I would work for God or simply be content to nuzzle the good life we had found.

If I went into ministry full-time, how would I support my family? Where would the money come from? I knew the Lord could provide, but would He? Was this really what He wanted for me? I felt I needed some confirmation. I remembered Gideon in the Bible and how he used a fleece for confirmation of the call of God. So I kept praying, "Lord, I need a fleece for this call to the ministry, but I don't know what to ask You for."

## FLEECE

About this time, a woman I knew called to invite me to speak at her church. "Jim," she said apologetically, "we really want you to come, but the time we have available is the Fourth of July weekend. With the holiday, there will probably be fewer than twenty people in attendance. We'll understand if you don't want to come for so few people."

As she spoke, the prompting of the Lord came to me, saying, "This is your fleece if you want it, Jim."

So I said, "Of course, I'll come."

Then, turning to God in prayer, I said, "Lord, if You've really called me to speak to people full-time, I want there to be people for me to speak to. I don't think that thirty or even forty people would be a miracle, so I am asking You to bring fifty people—two and a half times the number she said would be there."

I was the first person at the church that day. I was motivated. I wanted to see how the Lord was going to answer my prayer. Had He really called me to be a minister? Sally and I sat near the front as people came in, and by the time I got up to speak, there were eight in the church. "Well, Lord," I said silently, "I guess I got my answer."

The door opened just then, and a family of four came in. "That's still only twelve, Lord." Another three people came in. "That's fifteen." Then two more and a family of four brought the number to twenty-one. Soon it was twenty-eight, then thirty-four, forty, and forty-three.

I was trying to preach, but inside I was in turmoil. I tried to follow my sermon notes, but it wasn't easy to count and preach at the same time. I'm sure the people must have wondered what was wrong with me, as surely I was distracted. I kept thinking, *This can't be happening,* and yet it was.

The numbers continued to climb: forty-eight and then fifty-one, then sixty. I was still preaching and counting, but it didn't stop. The next thing I knew, it was seventy-three and soon climbed to seventy-eight. Finally, I gave up. I cried out in my heart, "Lord, I quit counting! I have my answer!" Still the people came until the little church was full.

Well, I preached my heart out to those people. I was on fire because I knew that this was what God had called me to do. After the sermon, I asked everyone I could, "Why did you come today?"

"We had no intention of coming today," one told me. "We just didn't feel like going camping as we had planned."

"I don't know," said another. "We just felt that we had to be here today."

"We had other plans," one couple shared, "but someone called us and said, 'There is this fellow coming to church this week. We heard a tape of his, and it was really good! He's coming over sixteen hundred miles and is only going to be here one day. Change your plans, you've got to come.' So, we changed our plans and came."

And so the stories went of unexpected phone calls or last-minute cancellations of prior commitments. Only I knew the real reason they had come. God was speaking to me through their actions. "Jim, you asked for fifty, but I'm giving you more than fifty. I want you to work for Me!"

As I talked with those dear people on their way out of church, I thought repeatedly, *What a God I serve!* "Lord, You're asking me to go out and be a fisher of men, and here I stand. I am not trained by any literary institution of the world but trained up in the wilderness by Your Spirit. Lord, what do You want me to teach them?"

"Jim, I want you to teach them the practical gospel of how to walk by faith. Teach them how to abide in Me, how to live by grace, and how to apply that in their daily lives: to their marriages, to their families, to their churches, and to their contacts with the world. Let them understand the basis of the gospel, which is a living experience in Me. Let them understand that this is to be their experience moment by moment, hour by hour, day by day.

"And Jim, as it is recorded in Revelation 12:11: 'And they overcame him by the blood of the Lamb and by the word of their testimony'(NKJV), your preaching is not to be like the common preaching that is so popular in the churches today. You are to preach from your own personal testimony—to incorporate the power of Christ in you, the hope of glory, at every opportunity. Thus every sermon you give is to hold up the blood of the Lamb before the people.

"Jim, you are not to love this wonderful life you have found with Me in the mountains. Rather, I want you to forsake the life you have found for the benefit of others. I am calling you to spend time away from your mountain retreat to share your testimony with others that they, too, may find the practical gospel and that it may transform their lives as yours has been transformed."

I went to bed that night, knowing the Lord was asking me to forsake the lucrative real estate practice with which He had so blessed me. However, when I awoke the next morning at 4:30, I sat there in bed with the Bible on my lap, shaking. The wonderful emotional experience of my answered prayer was over, and now I was dealing with reality. Would I actually do it?

## A SECOND FLEECE

Finally, I said, "Lord, Gideon had a second fleece. And Lord, if I am to never look back at this moment, if I am never going to regret this decision, I need a second fleece. Lord, this is a tough call. I mean, this is a no-looking-back decision. This is the rest of my life, to never do another thing but this that You have asked me to do. I have never done anything like it before. I want You to confirm in Your Word my calling to the gospel ministry."

Now that is a hard thing to ask because no verse in the Bible says, "Jim Hohnberger, you are to become a minister of the gospel."

There I sat with my Bible. I prayed and searched my heart to make sure there was nothing between myself and God. Having done that, I started leafing through the Bible, page by page, for almost an hour until I came to the book of Ephesians, chapter 3. It was as if the Holy Spirit shook me and said, "This is the right place."

"Lord, I feel impressed I should read here."

"Start on the right column, Jim."

My eyes fell onto verse 7: "Whereof I was made a minister, according to the gift of the grace of God given unto me by the effectual working of his power" (KJV).

I had shivers from my head to my toes! Wow! Talk about confirmation! Now I knew God had called me and that His grace would sustain me. I sat there in bed with the tears running down my face until Sally woke up. I told her all that had happened and how she had been a part of it even though she had no idea at the time. She was with me 100 percent. What a gem! I had been right about her reaction all along.

The call of God upon the heart is often unknown to those about us. You may be the only one who knows what God is asking of you at this moment. Even your spouse may not know what the pivotal point in your life is, but you do. Whatever it is, you must deal with it. Today, as you read these lines, you are choosing—even if your choice is simply to put off that choice. All of us need to understand that when we decide not to make a choice, in essence our choice is to reject that which God is asking us to do.

"Sally," I said, "when we get home, I will no longer be in real estate. I can't sell my real estate practice because God has asked me to give it to another man."

This Christian man and his family had moved to our area from California. They didn't have much, and the man was trying to get on his feet. I could have sold that real estate practice with all its listings for tens of thousands of dollars. But God told me to give it to this other family and to commit to work with that man every week for a year, so he could give his family the same opportunity God had given me.

I had argued, "Lord, someone would give me fifty or sixty thousand dollars for that practice. I mean, that could be my nest egg. That's money I could use to support myself for the next couple of years while You get this ministry thing going."

But the Lord said, "No, Jim. Your dependence needs to be on Me and not a nest egg in the bank."

So I went home and told the other family my story. They prayed about it, and a week later, I started training him to sell real estate. It took about two months before he was settled and I could move on to my once-a-week commitment. By September, I was ready to ask, "Lord, what do I do? Here I am, send me."

## BEGINNINGS

A call came from California asking me to come and work with five or six families who were having trouble. "This is your first call, Jim," the Lord told me. I went gladly, and we worked with those families. I came home feeling really high because for the first time, those families came to understand the practical gospel and were starting to apply it to their lives. As they began to make even little changes, they experienced the wonderful results of living by principle and cooperating with God.

I was invited to a friend's house to talk with a man who was visiting. This man was a minister, and while I didn't know it at that time, he was shortly going to host a gathering of more than fifty ministers from around the world. They talked with me about the problems in the churches and what they felt the solutions would be.

I couldn't agree with them. I shared with them that the issues of doctrine and practice were only symptoms of the real problem, which was that the churches have completely lost sight of the practical gospel that is able to transform the life. I didn't expect it, but this minister told me of their upcoming meeting and asked if I would be willing to give the opening and closing addresses to the visiting ministers.

I will never forget the sermon I preached that day titled "Who Am I?" I shared with those ministers that they were completely inadequate to do the work they were called to do, and they needed continual dependence upon God. By the time I finished that opening address, the men were in tears, and my sermon had changed the focus of the whole conference.

After this conference, calls to speak came from Europe, New Zealand, England, and all over the United States. I had wondered where the calls were going to come from. God knew. The calls poured in as those men from the conference shared my name around the world.

We can accept only a handful of the requests we receive. Since that day, we have spoken in fourteen different countries and in all but five states. Magazine articles followed, and I was privileged to share the gospel on satellite television. So I set my hand to the work and have never turned away to this day.

What about you, my friends? Have you turned away? Is there something in your life right now that God is asking you to surrender to Him, some pivotal point where you are holding out on God? Don't put it off. Everything must inevitably be faced someday. Won't you resolve it right now?

Often I end a series of meetings by asking those attending what they are going to do with the messages they have heard. This is a deeper question than asking if they believe; actions are always the outgrowth of true belief. My heart has been thrilled and tears have often come from my eyes as countless families have committed to making the gospel a practical reality in their lives. I ask them publicly because this public statement encourages others while it cements the decisions they've made in their hearts.

So I am asking you to write down the pivotal point in your life that God is asking you to surrender to Him. Use the form at the end of the chapter, or if you want, write it down on a separate sheet of paper. In any case, choose today, for now is the hour, and every time we come up to a decision and back away from it, it becomes easier to refuse the next time.

## MY PIVOTAL POINT WITH GOD

Lord, I realize that I have had a standoff with You in the following area.

_____

_____

_____

_____

I surrender it to You today!
Your Child,

_____
Signature

*Chapter Twelve*

# THE HESITANT ONE

You almost persuade me to become a Christian.
*Acts 26:28 NKJV*

I KNEW WALT'S island was supposed to be a beautiful place. Still, the sight of it made my pulse quicken with delight. The rhythmic movement of the paddles and the quiet sound of lake water dripping off the blades seemed completely in harmony with our peaceful surroundings.

Shaped somewhat like a volcano, the rounded island rose steeply from the lake. Its foliage occasionally granted our interested gaze a glimpse of the lake home, deepening our anticipation. We had been looking forward to this trip for some time. This island was to be our vacation home until the following Monday.

My family needed the time away. The pressures of travel and ministry had motivated me to think about our need for rest and relaxation, activities that were increasingly hard to do at home. We could and certainly did turn off the phone when we needed a break. But even when intentionally set aside, household jobs and ministry correspondence have a way of exerting their own pressures.

Because of this, I finally approached my friend about using his island. Walt was indeed both friend and mentor to me in my real estate practice, but I had never asked him anything like this before:

"Walt, my family is stressed out! We need a place where we can go to just rest and relax, a place where nobody knows how to reach us. Could we use your island? Oh, and Walt, while we are there, is there some type of project you need done—some type of repairs or cleanup we can do for you? That way, we can be givers and not just takers."

He was visibly pleased. "I've never done this before," he said, "but then no one has ever been willing to do something in return for me either. They all just want to use the island. Jim, I'd be delighted to let your family spend some time there, and I'm sure we can find something for you to do."

My reminiscing ended abruptly as the canoe slid alongside the dock. After carrying our baggage up the hill to the delightful lake home, Sally and I headed back down to the dock. "Boys," I instructed, "you make the meal, and when it's ready, come down to the dock and get us. We're going to sit in the sun."

This might seem a little strange for a father to say to his ten- and twelve-year-old sons, but we had learned to turn the kitchen duties over to the boys. In far too many families, the mother is practically a servant to the children. No husband should allow such a situation to continue. The whole family must help to lift the burden of the household tasks from the mother. If they do this, the family will find that not only will the children learn important lessons of home maintenance, but they gain a mother, and the husband a wife, who has time and energy to play with them and share their lives.

Try lifting from your wife or from your mother any burdens that other family members can bear, and you will find your efforts more than repaid in the loving attention that she can now invest in you and the other members of her family. If the family will redeem those energies that were once consumed in everyday household tasks, everyone benefits.

I am very mindful that the wife and mother is the heart of the home, and the surest recipe for happiness is for the woman who plays such a crucial role to have the energy and enthusiasm to fulfill her God-given mission.

My boys, as usual, prepared a wonderful meal. Then, with a little free time before the time we normally ate, they set off to explore the island.

Relaxing at the dock was an awfully easy thing to do in such a conducive setting. The clear, jade waters reflected the sun until it seemed that each tiny wavelet was crowned with shining diamonds, which sparkled as they moved. Peace, contentment, and quiet conversation came naturally as we enjoyed the chance to reconnect with each other.

Suddenly, the sounds of footsteps thundered down the steep stairs that led up from the dock to the rest of the island. Matthew and Andrew raced toward us, chattering incessantly with all the excitement and enthusiasm only ten- and twelve-year-old boys can possess.

"Father, Mother, you've got to come see them!"

"We've got to see what?"

"Diving boards!"

Gradually, we found out from the boys that on the west side of the island were some tall cliffs. On those cliffs were some diving boards. One was about as high as a one-story house and the other was as high as a two-story house. The boys were as excited as they could be about these boards. Deep down inside, they wanted to jump off them, but they were still young enough that they wouldn't unless their father led the way.

"Can you go off them, Father?"

"Of course, I can," I responded without much thought.

"Let's go!" they exclaimed.

"Wait a minute! Just hold on a minute!" I said. "I think we ought to have lunch first, then maybe we can go over to the other side of the island and look at those boards."

In truth, I was hesitating. I knew I could jump off those boards. I had been off high boards before, so I knew I would not get hurt. I knew that Walt had put those boards there for a reason, so there was no fear that the water wasn't deep enough. My boys wanted to see me go, and I wanted to please my sons, but still I hesitated. I wasn't all that sure I wanted to go through with it.

## THE BIG MOMENT!

After lunch, the boys did the dishes—in record time, I might add. This was going to be a big adventure. They came to me and said, "Are you ready to go off those boards, Father?"

I was still hesitant, so I stalled for time. "When I was growing up," I told them, "I was always told you should wait at least an hour after eating before you swim to prevent cramps. I'll go in an hour."

Now, I must confess that I have no idea if that fact is true, and I doubt that I would have been inclined to abide by such a rule if I had wanted to go off those boards. Under the circumstances, it was just an excuse, a rationalization giving me permission to avoid making a decision. My boys were disappointed at another delay, but when an hour had passed, they were right back with the same question. "Are you ready to go now, Father?"

"OK," I said. "Let's go."

They were off to the other side of the island as if I had shot them out of a cannon. Sally and I walked a little slower. When we arrived at the diving boards, where do you think my boys were standing? By the lowest board? Not in the least! They were by the highest board. "Up here, Father!" they called.

"All right, I'm coming."

Climbing to the highest board, I walked out to the edge and looked once more at the beautiful jade waters of this mountain lake. When you stand at the end of a diving board, it seems twice as far down to the water as it looks from below. As I stood there looking down, my boys were shouting instructions to me that went something like this: "Jump! Jump! Jump! Why don't you jump?"

"Just give me a minute to appraise the situation. I'm going to count to ten," I told them, "and then I'm going to go off."

The boys caught hold of this idea and, seeing a way to hurry me along, began to count for me in an incredibly speedy fashion. "One, two, three, four, five, six, seven . . ."

"*Whoa!*" I called out to them. "I'll do my own counting. Thanks anyway."

So there I was, torn between two desires, two loves. On the one hand I loved my boys, wanted to please them, wanted to fulfill their expectations, to be their hero. But my self-will was loathe to cast fear aside and take that step. So there I stood, suspended between the heavens above and the green waters below.

Intellectually, I knew others had taken the step off that board, and it was possible for me to do the same. I desired to make the jump not only for myself, but to encourage my boys. The battle raged because I had to choose to go off the board of my own volition, that is, through the exercise of my own free will. And this is just the conflict we face when called to surrender to the will of God.

## THE LAST GREAT STEP

Whenever we are brought to the choice between what self-will wants and what we know God is calling us to, there is a conflict. And the common reaction to this conflict is hesitation. We know God is calling us to an experience of full surrender, yet we hesitate.

We know that others have taken that step of full dependence on Him. We know that God never fails those who trust Him, and still we hold back.

In many ways, we are like the children of Israel after leaving slavery in Egypt. They had left one life behind but had not yet entered the promised land. We, too, have a long road left to travel in our pursuit of God. Perhaps we left bad habits or bad associates behind us. Maybe doctrinal errors or traditional understandings fell by the wayside. Then again, we may have turned away from worldly entertainment, music, and fashions only to find out that truthfully, while we may have come out of our pasts, we have failed to enter our futures—walking with God every moment of every hour of every day and teaching others to do the same.

Looking back at my life, I see that my steps toward this goal of full surrender have been by increment rather than one big step. It has been this way in my life not because God willed it that way but because it was the manner in which I would respond. My life could be broken into four stages.

1. First, I was ruled by self with no influence from God. I did my thing, my way.
2. Second, I allowed God some control while self still ruled.
3. Third, I moved deeper in my walk with God, and there was less of self and more of God ruling and controlling.
4. Fourth and last, all of God and none of me.

## HESITATING

What is God saying to you right now on your diving board? I know you are hesitating over something. Likely, it has something to do with the issue you wrote out in the last chapter. Or perhaps it's a sensitive area God brought to your mind when you looked at that commitment form, but you were afraid to give it to God or even to admit to yourself it was there.

You desire to surrender this sensitive area, but it's hard to believe that you'll be happy if you let it go. This is Satan's greatest lie. He has deceived all of us into believing that we can be happy only when we get our own way. Don't trust your feelings. Instead, act on principle. Your intellect must decide that you will no longer allow feelings and emotions to control.

If you do this, you will discover that you have unlocked the secret of a happy Christian life. You will find, as I have, that the very step from which you drew back was the path to peace and happiness.

That's just what I found when I jumped off that diving board! It was great. I screamed and yelled and cheered all the way down. When I hit that refreshingly cool water, I felt more alive than ever before. I climbed out and went off the board again and again.

Matthew came up to me and asked tentatively, "Do you think I could go off, Father?"

"Of course, you can," I answered.

So he got up on that board and went though his own hesitating process. Finally, he did it. I could see he was scared, but he held himself bravely and entered the water just as straight as an arrow.

Then Andrew came up to me and said "Father, I want to go off that board, but I'm scared. Will you go with me?"

"I sure will, son. Give me your hand. I'll be with you all the way."

He was scared to death! I didn't push him but stood with him while he worked through his own hesitation. Then I let him count, and we jumped. I wish you could have seen the grin on that boy's face. You would have thought he had conquered the world!

Then all three of us turned to Sally. But she taught us all a lesson in bravery. "If you're going, I'm going!" And she did!

All of us learned to overcome our hesitation and gain the victory over those feelings and emotions that try to hold us back. The true Christian life is like that board. It often requires a leap of faith, a decision that we're not going to turn back, just as we couldn't get back on that board after stepping off. We were committed! This is what God is looking for in each of us.

Go ahead!

Leap out and take that last great step. You cannot fail!

# Chapter Thirteen

# FAILURE IS NOT AN OPTION

With men it is impossible, but not with God;
for with God all things are possible.
*Mark 10:27* NKJV

SO MANY PEOPLE have asked me how they can achieve in their families the changes we have gained in ours that I can't even count them, but it must be thousands by now. Not all families are called to leave everything they know and move to the wilderness as we did. Indeed, most people are not called to such a life, and yet we all desire great spiritual awakenings in our lives. It is no easy task.

In fact, for most of us, the obstacles seem almost insurmountable and we despair of hope itself. I want to assure you from my own experience that the God I've come to know is a God of the impossible. Often what matters more than money, more than ability, more than natural aptitude is our *attitude*.

You can do this. You can have a wilderness experience with God even if you never set foot in the wilderness. And you can do this with the assurance that failure is not an option. The events that taught me this happened a long time ago, but I never tire of the story, for it is reflected in one form or another in every human life, sometimes echoing the heroic and, sadly, at times, demonstrating an all-too-human characteristic: to believe something is impossible often makes it so.

It was July 20, 1969, and NASA had just landed the first man on the moon. Do you remember the circumstances? My memories of it are so vivid that I can recall exactly where I was. I was returning home from a date in Milwaukee, Wisconsin, with my girlfriend, Sally. As I drove my convertible and listened to the news reports over the radio, I glanced up at the bright sphere of the moon and thought, *What an awesome event!*

The whole world was looking on as the first man walked on the moon. It was an accomplishment of historic proportions, equal perhaps to Christopher Columbus's discovering the New World.

For centuries, men had stared into the heavens and dreamed of traveling to the bright surface of the moon. As I was growing up, comic books and children's books, as well as movies and science-fiction novels, touted the idea of taking rocket ships to the moon. Now the United States, in response to President Kennedy's rousing speech, had at last met the lofty goal. He had placed before us as a people the challenge of putting man on the moon before the end of the decade. I couldn't help but feel the thrill of pride in my country and admiration for the brave men who had brought us into a new age.

It was a time of idealism that crossed international boundaries. These men were more than just American citizens; they were envoys of all mankind, so aptly reflected in Neil Armstrong's immortal words, "One small step for man, one giant leap for mankind."

Upon return, the crew was given a heroes' welcome in city after city. But on April 11, 1970, another spacecraft was launched toward the moon, and I doubt any of you remember it. By that point, space flight had become routine—so much so that none of the TV networks provided live coverage of the launch. Newspapers buried the story many pages away from the headlines.

The media was, after all, reflecting the attitude of the public, which, as a whole, had little interest in the mission of what were to be the fifth and sixth men to walk on the moon. The public's attention span, capricious at best, had proven that one can get used to the most stunning of events if exposed to them often enough.

The truth was that no one outside of the space program took much notice of this particular flight until a short, poignant radio message crackled down, slightly delayed because of its passage through miles of space: "Houston, we have a problem."

More than two hundred thousand miles into their mission, astronauts Fred Haise, Jack Swigert, and mission commander Jim Lovell found themselves in the *Apollo XIII* command module facing a situation no one, especially the men inside, believed could ever occur.

Many insiders at NASA considered the *Apollo* command module to be almost indestructible, yet something had gone desperately wrong in its fuel cells, and the men were losing electrical power. The cells were a marvel in both technology and simplicity. Two gases were combined with the help of electrodes and, thanks to the God-designed principles of physics, these supplied the command module with three things the astronauts could not long do without: heat, water, and electricity. If the astronauts' fuel cells went out, they would lose not only these consumables, but their oxygen supply as well, since the same tanks that supplied the fuel cells supplied the cabin oxygen.

It all started with a mysterious bang, and suddenly a main power circuit's undervoltage alarm sounded. This was critical enough, but if the other circuit (or *bus*) failed, the men would face almost certain death. Soon it appeared that the other bus might indeed fail, and the crew joined with mission control in a desperate struggle to save their lives and bring their crippled ship back home.

News of the disaster was broadcast, and television commentators estimated the men's odds for survival at no better than one in ten. Even NASA, whose news releases were always known to be optimistic, conceded that the astronauts' lives were threatened.

## CRIPPLED LIVES

Today, we face a similar situation as the God of the universe desperately battles to bring us home from this planet. To do this, He must repair our crippled lives. I am not speaking of the lives in the world but of those who are already within Christian churches.

Christians are supposed to have the power to bring the gospel to the world, but today we have lost our fuel cells, and we are powerless to do the job. Just like the *Apollo XIII* mission so long ago, we are broken. Something has gone dreadfully wrong in each of our lives, and while the specifics may vary, we are all stranded here on our spacecraft—the earth—with a determined self-will and human nature. These will, if left to their own desires, destroy us. Because the problem in their spacecraft was quite literally behind them, the astronauts of *Apollo XIII* could not see what had gone so very wrong; like those astronauts, we may have no true conception of exactly what has happened to cause our problems.

Yet lack of knowledge did not prevent the astronauts from cooperating with mission control, and in exactly the same manner, God needs your cooperation. He desperately needs your cooperation if He is to save you and your crew from certain destruction!

As the crew and ground control of *Apollo XIII* examined the data streaming back from their sensors, their first impulse was to discount it. It was so bad that they thought it must be an instrumentation problem—no way things could have gone that wrong. It is the most human of responses, and as I have traveled the globe, I have met countless thousands who have the data telling them they are endangered, but they discount it. Unless we shake off this attitude and become willing to think outside of our own expectations, we will never be in a position to take the steps necessary to prevent our destruction and that of the ones we love.

It is perhaps the greatest tribute to the NASA engineers that, gradually, those brilliant men, whose expertise was the ability to send spacecraft more than a quarter million miles to the moon and back, drew the conclusion that the command module was dying, and when it died, it would take the three fragile creatures inside with it.

As horrible as the thoughts of a dead crew were, the future of space flight looked even bleaker. The ship wouldn't disappear but would enter a permanent orbit around the earth forever reminding men of their failure. With such a specter before the crew and mission control, it was little wonder that rumors flew fast and furious that this might be NASA's greatest disaster. People all around the world were horrified at the idea of astronauts dying in space with no escape possible.

Once the members of mission control drew the correct conclusions about what they were seeing and properly understood the gravity of the situation, they had to make hard decisions, choices that made everyone uncomfortable because they seemed so extreme.

What about you, my friend? Have you been facing any hard decisions? I know what you face is hard when you examine the task of entering this experience. I know because those decisions were hard for me to make more than two decades ago when I faced them. Are you willing to do whatever it takes, or will you stubbornly cling to your own personal dreams and wishes?

For *Apollo XIII*, the plan to land on the moon had to be scrapped. Those men had trained much of their lives to fulfill the dream of walking on the moon, but they had to set it aside just to try to get home alive. They knew it had to be done, but it didn't alter their disappointment, nor will the certainty that you are doing what's best remove all your disappointments.

When I decided to move away from the influences of the city

life, of family and friends, my wife and I had to give up all that we had ever aspired to. We were up-and-coming professionals with a large income and great reputations. Yet to bring salvation's benefits practically into our lives, we decided that we would have to give it all up. We gave up our hope of professional success. We gave up our dreams of material prosperity. And we gave up our hopes of ever finding worldly notoriety. Like the crew of *Apollo XIII*, we determined to do whatever we had to do! You may find, as I did, that you have to give up your career, your fortunes, your current occupation, and your current home. It may even require you to give up your toys. You may also find you have to make relatively few changes compared with us, or maybe more. Remember, we are not to follow others; this is *God* leading you, not *me* leading you. In fact, it may take everything you have to gain a real, lasting, and practical connection with God.

## LIFEBOAT

There was only one hope for the *Apollo XIII* crew, and mission control quickly implemented it. The lunar excursion module, or LEM, would have to be used as a sort of lifeboat, if you will, to sustain the crew's lives until they could return to Earth. They had less than two hours to power up the ship and transfer the data before the command module died.

It was a hectic and stressful time for the crew. They not only had to set up the LEM but also shut down the command module so that, hopefully, they could restart it and use it for reentry. Escaping the situations that are dragging you down may seem just as complex and difficult.

Once the transfer was complete, mission control and the crew breathed a sigh of relief, but only a slight one, for all those involved knew they couldn't sustain the drain they were putting on the

LEM's batteries and life-support system. They had merely moved from a ship, in which they were sure to die in the next couple of hours, to one in which they could not survive more than the next couple of days.

NASA called emergency meetings, and experts grappled with the challenge. Oxygen was a problem. The lithium hydroxide filter used to remove the carbon dioxide from the air would run out in less than two days. The command module had more lithium hydroxide filters, but they were designed for a totally different system.

If that problem could be solved, the power supply became the real obstacle. No matter how many ways they looked at it, there just wasn't enough power to make it home. Examining the figures, both NASA engineers and the crew concluded they would have to find some other way to run their spacecraft.

Have you drawn the same conclusion? Too many of us have moved out of the world, out of certain death, into the apparent safety of the church, only to realize later that all we have done is delay destruction—not prevent it.

In the NASA structure, the senior flight controller was in charge of all flight decisions, and no one could overrule him. Gene Kranz was that powerful man. He pulled his control team off the monitors and assembled them in a vacant conference room. Basically, he told them that he hadn't lost a spacecraft yet, and he wasn't planning to start now. He wanted options—and lots of them—to bring the men home. Failure, he told them, was not an option.

## ATTITUDE

What is your attitude? Have you accepted a crippled connection to God? Is your life fractured and broken? This was my experience, and I longed for something better—something that would actually save me from myself.

I have, throughout the chapters of this book, shared with you the struggles, the victories, and the defeats on my way to gaining a walk with God. Over and over, I have found that I was my own worst enemy. Nothing anyone has ever done to me has been as harmful as those things I have done to myself. You see, I have a tendency to let self rule in my life, and when it does, it affects my attitude. I might have been enthusiastic about letting God control my life in the morning, but I was less excited in the afternoon when the Lord allowed a problem to beset me.

My attitude altered everything: my outlook on life—*Oh, I'm sure things are going to get worse before they get better*—my view of my Christian experience—*I can never get control over my temper*—even my view of my wife and family—*If only Sally did this or that differently,* or *If only the boys minded better, then I'd be happier, and then I would find it easier to be a Christian.*

Do you believe that failure is not an option? God believes it. He says in Mark 10:27, "With men it is impossible, but not with God: for with God all things are possible" (KJV). God holds that attitude because it is true. Isaiah 42:4 describes Jesus by saying, "He shall not fail nor be discouraged" (KJV).

The first crisis we must conquer is our attitude. In the early days of Israel's monarchy, the Philistines were a constant menace. The armies of Israel were not up to the task of defeating the enemy and often had to resort to uneasy standoffs rather than outright victories. During one such engagement, the king's son, Jonathan, set out toward the enemy with only his armor bearer. Two men against an army? Yet he was convinced that God was going to act for them. The Philistines held the high ground—an advantage in any conflict—and Jonathan was not such a fool as to go marching into the enemy's camp on his own initiative.

Jonathan prayed God would fulfill certain conditions, namely, that when the enemy discovered them approaching, they would invite them up to their encampment. If this occurred, it would indicate God would deliver the Philistines into his hands. Sure enough, when the enemy saw the two lone men, they encouraged them to come up—obviously thinking them easy game.

But Jonathan and his armor bearer were no easy conquest, and the noise of battle soon brought the whole of Israel's force to the field of conflict where they won a decisive victory. Jonathan set out to do the impossible, believing that with God it *was* possible. His attitude was his most important weapon. (Read 1 Samuel 14:4–14 for the full account.)

What is your attitude? Are you with those who feel failure is likely and victory too difficult to obtain?

Time is critical, my friend. The longer mission control struggled to decide what to do, the less power the module would have when it came time to try the solution. How long before you decide to make your personal walk with God a priority and everything else subordinate? If you fail to decide, you have decided.

## HOUSTON, WE HAVE A PROBLEM

Two decades ago, Sally and I decided we had a problem. We decided it wasn't going to be fixed unless we took some drastic action. We had been in the church and considered ourselves Christians, but we didn't know how to walk or talk with God. I was the head elder, but if I could have given all the people in my community my religious experience, they would have still been yelling at their wives and getting irritated at their children. It wasn't until I admitted to myself, and then to God, that I had a problem that I had a chance for healing to take place.

I had come into the church, and the church had told me I was converted, that I was spiritual, but in truth I was doing everything in the power of Jim Hohnberger and not in the power of God. I was self-directed, and the vast majority of those in the churches are exactly the same as I was: sincere, but self-directed. They are getting along in the power of their knowledge and their reforms, but they are not empowered by a living connection with Jesus.

That's why it is so easy for us to pick on the faults of others but so hard to look at our own lives. We don't like admitting, even to ourselves, the idea that something might be deeply and fundamentally flawed in our experience. Yet, as I looked at myself, I had to draw the conclusion that I had a problem. I came to see that without dramatic changes, I was a lost man in spite of my church offices, reputation, or theology. We are crippled Christians, and yet we think we are OK.

It was not until I realized just how crippled and in need of a deeper experience with God we were that my entire focus became the same as that of the *Apollo XIII* crew: to get back home. Sally and I determined to go back to God at all costs. We set our sights high and set out to achieve the impossible. We wanted to give our family the best, and we wanted to protect ourselves from other influences as much as possible.

## SOLUTIONS OUTSIDE OF THE BOX

The NASA engineers who worked out solutions to the spacecraft's many problems faced opposition to their outside-of-the-box thinking. The solutions they had come up with were risky and seemed extremely careless to those who believed that the way they had always done things was the only safe way. The problem was that under the traditional methods, the astronauts would almost certainly have died.

Critics have ideas and objections and concerns, but what they all too often lack are solutions. The engineers who worked to save *Apollo XIII* faced such men, and so will you if you set out to try the unorthodox.

## COMMUNICATION

You will also face the difficulty of the task. When the engineers on the ground came up with a method to adapt the command module's filters, the crew had to build, in weightlessness, the item the engineers had developed—an item they had never seen before, using only the description of the capsule communicator, who was always another astronaut.

In like manner, you will be trying to rebuild your life after a pattern that you have not likely ever seen illustrated in the lives and homes of those about you. If you think this is difficult, you are correct. Only strong and vital communication with mission control enabled the astronauts to accomplish this project, and you will need this same living connection with God to succeed. What is your communication like with your Commander in Chief in heaven's mission control? Is it continual, or is it broken? Do you talk occasionally? Never? Do the day's activities sever your communication?

In my travels throughout the United States and thirteen other countries, it has shocked me to see how few who claim to be Christ's followers actually communicate with Him on an ongoing basis. This is serious because God says, "I will instruct thee and teach thee in the way which thou shalt go: I will guide thee with mine eye" (Ps. 32:8 KJV). How can He lead us if we are not listening?

If the astronauts of *Apollo XIII* hadn't maintained contact with mission control, they would have been lost. The men aboard *Apollo XIII* waited eagerly for every instruction, often looking for information that mission control had not yet prepared. Why were they so insistent? Because life itself depended upon the data they received.

Do you wait that eagerly for God to tell you what to do?

## FOLLOW-THROUGH

The crew of *Apollo XIII* had to put into effect the changes ground control asked for, and these were extremely difficult. But the astronauts allowed mission control complete management of their destiny.

Many of us have given God *some* management in our lives, and our lives are a mess because God can't do a whole lot without complete control. Aboard the spacecraft, the crew had to drastically reduce power use. In the lunar excursion module, the men eliminated all nonessential as well as some essential items. The astronauts gave up heat, they could no longer vent wastes, and water was in tight enough supply that the crew had to think carefully before taking even a sip. Their food froze. Their bodies shivered, and the lack of water caused one of them a kidney infection and fever. But they could endure all if this was the price of saving their lives and returning home.

What God asks of many of you may not be comfortable, but it is for your survival. You are in a life-and-death situation, and everything is at stake in your compliance with mission control.

Throughout the flight, the crew had to readjust its course for a tiny degree of drift in the flight path. In the same way, as we begin to drift off God's flight plan, He will let us know, and it will be up to us to correct our travel. I can't count how many times God has had to get my attention and let me know I was drifting off course. You will likely find the same is true. It is easy to drift; what matters is our response to the heavenly messages. The longer we delay course correction, the harder the task of realignment.

## COURAGE

Then there is courage. It takes courage in the face of discouraging odds to take the attitude that "failure is not an option." If courageous, daring men had not been part and parcel of the NASA team, that crew would have been lost. The crew of *Apollo XIII* demonstrated a positive response to a difficult situation and a resolve to carry out their task to the end when the odds seemed totally against them. We must have the same boldness if we are to succeed, and succeed we must!

On April 17, 1970, the crew of *Apollo XIII* splashed down in the Pacific Ocean. The president and the families of the crew flew on *Air Force One* to the South Pacific to greet these brave astronauts.

In the celebrations that followed, their mission to the moon was not even considered. The mission as planned was a failure, but in the massive team effort to save the crew, this failure became one of NASA's greatest moments of success. The crew was saved, and the world cheered! Praise God! I hope someday to complete the mission God has given me.

## SPLASHDOWN

On my desk sits a signed photograph of Gene Kranz, his signature in gold ink across the bottom. It is there to remind me—when I am tempted to get discouraged or anytime I feel the task before me is just too hard—failure is not an option! My God has already won the victory over all the powers that try to oppress me. He has a solution for my every difficulty, my every discouragement. He stands by, longing to help me, hoping and desiring that I just ask.

God would place at my disposal all the forces of heaven if need be, yet, all too often, I have bemoaned my lot in life and given way to fears of destruction. We fail when failure need not be an option. I say this as one who has been there, not to point my finger at anyone else. I also say this as one who is learning that when I place my dependence upon the God of heaven, I *cannot* fail.

So, if you try God's way, what do have you to lose? He will

never force you to serve Him. If you find you are not happier, your marriage isn't sweeter, or your family isn't more at peace, He leaves you free to turn your back on Him and do things your own way.

Even if you have ignored Him for years, He stands ever ready to help you the minute you are willing to let Him. I can tell you that while I have not always followed all of His instructions perfectly, I am working in His strength to keep my sin-crippled craft on the heavenly flight plan. I hope and pray you will do the same.

If you do this, someday, not long from now, you and I shall see a city whose gates are set with pearls, whose streets are paved with gold. Outside the gates, I imagine the wide-spreading plains will swell into hills of beauty with majestic mountains rearing their lofty summits. With my wife and children, my son's wives and their children beside me, I want to explore those peaceful hills and living springs. I want to walk with my sons through heaven's gate and see them receive crowns of life from Christ's own hand.

And as I gather my family—my crew—in a giant hug, I want to shout, "Sally, Matthew, Andrew—and all of *you* too—we're home!"

# EPILOGUE

MORE THAN TWO decades have passed since we moved our family to the wilderness. Our little boys became big boys and then teenagers until today they stand in the fullness of manhood. Now the perspective of time permits me to look back at the last twenty-two years of my life that are the focus of this book.

You have spent a lot of time with me to this point, for which I am grateful, reading about my experiences and understandings. Had I been around when the Wright brothers first invented their airplane, I would have listened to their stories and their understandings as well, yet I would have had one final question before I tried out their invention: does it fly? It is a fair question, and you, dear reader, may have a similar question for me: will the surrendered life you have lived and experienced work just as well for me?

With the passage of time, I can tell you conclusively that it can be done! The program we set out on to find God and to draw together as a family absolutely works! I am not recommending anything that we haven't proven both in our own lives and in the lives of hundreds of other families.

This way of life will work for you as well, whether you live in the wilderness, move to the country, or stay where you are and just apply the same principles.

Today, both Matthew and Andrew are married to lovely wives

and raising their own families. They are successful real estate brokers specializing in wilderness and country properties. Their characters, which were formed so painstakingly in the wilderness, have drawn the attention of many of their clients, and more than one has contacted me, wanting to know how in the world we managed to raise such outstanding young men.

The secret is simple: Sally and I didn't raise them. We allowed God to do so through our cooperation with Him. Therefore, while we rejoice with the boys in their successes, we are continually humbled by the knowledge that it has only been through the grace of God that our family has achieved such results.

At the time of this writing, our little log cabin near Glacier National Park is home only to Sally and me. We get together with the boys whenever we can. They still enjoy their parents' company. If anything, our communion today is sweeter. Sally, my queen, and I stand ready to encourage them through each stage of life that we are privileged to witness.

In continuation of our full-time ministry, we've founded Empowered Living Ministries. This nonprofit organization is committed to teaching others how to live the practical gospel so that it can transform and restore their marriages and their families just as it did ours. We truly believe that the very essence of the gospel of Christ is restoration and empowerment in Him.

So, what of the future? Have we achieved all we set out to accomplish in possessing a marriage that is second to none and learning to walk with God? Yes, and we have realized our goal of raising our boys as true Christians. But that is only a hint of the future. As a teen, Matthew was struck with the notion of finding a hidden lake way back in the Canadian wilderness. It became his dream, his goal, and it stayed with him for years. Eventually, he achieved his goal, and by the time we returned to civilization, he had already thought of new areas to explore, new adventures to experience.

This is how Sally and I view our future. The completion of one dream does not dim the vision of the next. Climbing one mountain reveals only more and greater heights to conquer. Within us burns the desire to see what lies beyond the next hill.

The experience of the Christian life is ever upward. There will always be new heights of selflessness and new depths of dying to self to explore. Each new experience brings with it increased duties and greater joys in the company of Christ, our constant Companion.

Yes, my friends, it flies! I assure you, it flies. The only remaining question is this—are you going to fly it?

# ACKNOWLEDGMENTS

No man is an island, and certainly no writer is. Foremost, I want to acknowledge that this is not my book. I possess neither the wisdom nor the ability to set any words to paper that might help others along the pathway to truly knowing God. It is with great wonder and gratitude that I write these final words, identifying the true author as my God, who is my Friend and my constant Companion.

God rarely does through divine agencies what He can accomplish through humans, and many have contributed, some unwittingly, to the completion of this manuscript. A special thanks to my wife, queen, and best friend, Sally, as well as my sons, Matthew and Andrew. Your support and encouragement have meant more to me than words can convey.

My colaborers, Tim and Julie Canuteson—you take my black and white and make it color. Todd Chobatar for all his help. Bruce Barbour for believing it could be done. And the editors and staff at Thomas Nelson Publishers for their insightful comments.

# ABOUT THE AUTHOR

**Jim Hohnberger** is the founder of Empowered Living Ministries, Inc., a speaking and teaching ministry dedicated to helping people simplify their lives and embrace an authentic relationship with God. A sought-after speaker and author, Jim travels extensively throughout the United States and around the world, teaching others how to walk with God, revitalize their marriages, and reconnect with their families. He and his wife, Sally, have two sons, both of whom are married with families of their own.

# Want to Know
# MORE About
# the Hohnbergers?

E mpowered Living Ministries is the outgrowth of Jim and Sally's experience with God. Located near Glacier National Park, the ministry office is here to serve your needs, whether it is to book a speaking engagement, request a media appearance, or order any of a large variety of resource materials including books, booklets, seminars on CD, or a special DVD series. For more information contact:

Empowered Living Ministries
3945 North Fork Road
Columbia Falls, MT 59912

EMPOWEREDLIVINGMINISTRIES.ORG

Phone 406-387-4333
Orders 877-755-8300
Fax 406-387-4336

If you have enjoyed this book, we highly recommend the DVD *Our Resting Place*. In it you'll have the opportunity to visit with Jim and Sally, peek into Sally's kitchen, stand where Jim met the grizzly, try Andrew's swing, as well as tour their wilderness home and property. More than just interviews with the whole family or an interesting sightseeing excursion, *Our Resting Place* offers fresh insights into the God-given principles and philosophy that started this family on its unique modern odyssey of escaping to God.

1988—Matthew and Andrew with Lonesome, the Pet Black Bear

1990—Andrew Feeding a Buck in Velvet

1990—The Jungle Gym Matthew Built

1991—The Hohnberger Family Backpacking

1990—Six Miles of
Paddling to a Six-Mile Hike

1990—Andrew and Matthew
Atop Long Knife Peak, Glacier
National Park

1995—Matthew (age 16) and
Andrew (age 14)

1995—The Hohnberger Family, left to
right: Andrew, Jim and Sally (ages 46),
Matthew

1999—Jim's Firewood

2000—Matthew
(age 22) with Angela

2000—Sally with Andrew
and Matthew

2002—Andrew and Sarah's
Wedding, Pictured with
Matthew and Angela

2004 Open House

Special Music for 2004 Open House—Jim with Sons and Their Wives

The Hohnberger Home

2005 Open House